A TALE OF TWO OMARS

A Tale of Two Omars

A MEMOIR OF FAMILY, REVOLUTION, AND COMING OUT DURING THE ARAB SPRING

Omar Sharif Jr.

COUNTERPOINT

Berkeley, California

A Tale of Two Omars

Grateful acknowledgment is made to the following for permission to publish
reprinted material:
"Coming Out Story: We're Not in Cairo Anymore" © 2012 by *The Advocate*.

Library of Congress Cataloging-in-Publication Data
Names: Sharif, Omar, Jr., author.
Title: A tale of two Omars : a memoir of family, revolution, and coming out
    during the Arab Spring / Omar Sharif, Jr..
Description: First hardcover edition. | Berkeley : Counterpoint Press, 2021.
Identifiers: LCCN 2020056858 | ISBN 9781640094987 (hardcover) | ISBN
    9781640094994 (ebook)
Subjects: LCSH: Sharif, Omar, 1932-2015—Family. | Sharif, Omar, Jr. |
    Motion picture actors and actresses—Egypt—Biography. | Motion picture
    actors and actresses—Canada—Biography. | Gay activists—Canada—
    Biography. | Gay men—Canada—Biography.
Classification: LCC PN2978.S5 S53 2021 | DDC 791.4302/80922 [B]—dc23
LC record available at https://lccn.loc.gov/2020056858

Jacket design by Dana Li
Book design by Jordan Koluch

COUNTERPOINT
2560 Ninth Street, Suite 318
Berkeley, CA 94710
www.counterpointpress.com

Printed in the United States of America

10 9 8 7 6 5 4 3 2 1

To my grandparents for shaping and molding me.

And to Diane for then offering this advice:
"Now, be *you*."

I'm not an activist; I'm just a person with a story.

OMAR SHARIF JR.

CONTENTS

A TALE OF TWO OMARS

Introduction

Published in *The Advocate*
March 16, 2012

I write this article in fear. Fear for my country, fear for my family, and fear for myself. My parents will be shocked to read it, surely preferring I stay in the shadows and keep silent, at least for the time being.

But I can't.

Last January, I left Egypt with a heavy heart. I traveled to America, leaving behind my family, friends, and compatriots who were in the midst of embarking on a heroic journey toward self-determination. Despite the sound of gunshots in the streets and the images of Anderson Cooper being struck repeatedly over the head on CNN, I left hopeful that I would return to find a more tolerant and equal society. While I benefited from a life of privilege being Omar Sharif's grandson, it was always coupled with the onerous guilt that such a position might have been founded upon others' sweat and tears.

One year since the start of the revolution, I am not as hopeful.

The troubling results of the recent parliamentary elections dealt secularists a particularly devastating blow. The vision for a freer, more equal Egypt—a vision that many young patriots gave their lives to see realized in Tahrir Square—has been hijacked. The full spectrum of equal and human rights are now wedge issues used by both the Supreme Council of the Egyptian Armed Forces and the Islamist parties, when they should be regarded as universal truths.

I write this article despite the inherent risks associated because as we stand idle at what we hoped would be the pinnacle of Egyptian modern history, I worry that a fall from the top could be the most devastating. I write, with healthy respect for the dangers that may come, for fear that Egypt's Arab Spring may be moving us backward, not forward.

And so I hesitantly confess: I am Egyptian, I am half Jewish, and I am gay.

That my mother is Jewish is no small disclosure when you are from Egypt, no matter the year. And being openly gay has always meant asking for trouble, but perhaps especially during this time of political and social upheaval. With the victories of several Islamist parties in recent elections, a conversation needs to be had and certain questions need to be raised. I ask myself: Am I welcome in the new Egypt?

Will being Egyptian, half Jewish, and gay forever remain mutually exclusive identities? Are they identities to be hidden?

While to many in Europe and North America mine might seem like trivial admissions, I am afraid this is not so in Egypt. I anticipate that I will be chastised, scorned, and most certainly threatened. From the vaunted class of Egyptian actor and personality, I might just become an Egyptian public enemy.

And yet I speak out because I am a patriot.

I am a patriot who remembers a pluralistic Egypt, where despite a lack of choice in the political sphere, society comprised a multitude of beliefs and backgrounds. I remember growing up knowing gay men and women who were quietly accepted by those around them in everyday society. The motto was simple: "Stay quiet, stay safe." Today, too many are staying quiet as the whole of Egyptian society moves toward this monolithic entity I barely recognize.

Last month I went for an afternoon run outside my home in Cairo. It was hot, and so I removed my T-shirt. I got the strange sense someone was watching. I felt a car begin to slow behind me, and a man began to shout that I could no longer go out in the streets shirtless in the new Egypt. With reticence, I put my T-shirt on and continued to run.

Today, I write.

I write this article because there are many back home without a voice, without a face, and without an outlet. I write this article because I am not unique in Egypt and because many will suffer if a basic respect for fundamental human rights and equality is not embraced by Egypt's new government. I write this article because as an Egyptian national newly acquainted with a land of freedom, I feel a certain privilege that I can finally express myself openly as well as artistically. I have a voice, and with it comes a responsibility to share it during this time of social and political change, no matter the risks.

I write this article as a litmus test, calling for a reaction. I challenge each of the parties elected to parliament to speak out, on the record, as to where they stand on respect for the rights of all Egyptians, regardless of gender, sexual orientation, or political belief. Do religious parties speak of moderation now only to consolidate power? Show us that your true intent is not to gradually eradicate the few civil liberties and safeguards that we currently have protected by convention, if not constitution.

I write this article to understand my own position in the new Egyptian paradigm. To a greater degree, though, I want to know where my newborn sister fits, my Coptic Christian friends, and the entire list of those who seek a basic guarantee of rights affirmed just to know they can live safely in Egypt. I want to know that we are not sliding downward on a slippery slope from secular(ish) society toward Islamic fundamentalist state.

I challenge foreign governments and NGOs present in Egypt today to comment and demand answers on equal and human rights from both the leaders of the revolution and the new government. I urge them to lend the Egyptian people and any future governments the support necessary to protect those at risk and strengthen our laws so that an admission like mine is not a sentence to prison, physical harm, or worse. Lend guidance in formulating a new constitution that protects the lives and liberty of all citizens, reminding them that while I know all too well that Egypt is not ready to adopt or accept equal rights for gays, it should nonetheless be included in the discussion. We learn from the entrenchment of constitutional principles in long-established Western democracies that if a group is excluded from the outset, it could be centuries before the issue is revisited.

I write this article as an open letter to my fellow Egyptian people, mailed from many miles away, commending them on how far they have come in how short a time. We must continue to run toward, not away from, the ideals that started us down this extraordinary path. After all of this, if we pursue a national agenda that does not respect basic human rights, we are no better than the architects of tyranny, contempt, and oppression toppled throughout the Arab Spring.

I want to have a place in the new Egypt.

I write asking for my inclusion.

1

Icon & Iconoclast

With a sudden gasp, my body involuntarily shot to a seated position, my heart pounding like I had just crossed a finish line. I frantically patted my bare chest, making sure I was awake from whatever bad dream I had, only to moisten my hands with sweat. Something didn't feel right. I reached for my phone to see if I had any urgent messages, discovering I'd only slept a few hours. It was 4:04 a.m., and this was not the way to begin my day. Accustomed to years of living in the shadows, I sluggishly got out of bed, only to pace around my dark apartment wondering what had jolted me out of a deep sleep. I couldn't remember anything, so I shifted my focus to my itinerary for the day.

July in New York was merciless with its escalating heat waves and drenching humidity. I'd already sifted through my closet the night before in preparation for my interview, selecting a salmon-colored linen suit with a white shirt and crochet necktie. That afternoon,

I had an appointment with the executive director of a major phil-
anthropic foundation with the declared mission of advancing social
justice and conservation issues. The organization presented an ex-
cellent opportunity—and one that I needed. I'd spent the previous
two years as a national spokesperson for the world's largest LGBTQ
media advocacy organization. I thought it was time to solicit a grant
so that I could independently continue my accidental activism. It had
taken me a long time not only to discover but also to openly confess
who I was without reluctance. I was naive not to have considered the
controversy it would spark, but hopeful my confession would bring
change in repressive areas around the world, like Egypt, my home. I
was in Canada in March of 2012 when I settled my internal struggles
and added my voice to those calling for a more open and inclusive
Egypt. I wrote a letter revealing a lifelong secret: *I'm gay.*

I didn't think my letter in *The Advocate,* the world's leading
LGBTQ news source, would travel as fast as it did, but it went viral.
My intent was for my words to reach eyes around the world because
the need for change was real. Tolerance and acceptance were long
overdue. My mistake was that I hadn't anticipated the tsunami of
hate in the aftermath. Yet, as painful as it was, after embarking on
that journey, nothing could make me recoil into the isolation and
loneliness I'd spent a lifetime trying to escape. I found it necessary to
continue creating opportunities and providing hope for people like
me, those fearfully struggling to live openly and authentically. I discarded the mask I'd worn and finally used my voice to live out loud,
which allowed me to discover the power in speaking the truth, while
letting others make their own conciliations.

I'd grown up in a family in which both sides had made significant
contributions to social consciousness. I'd experienced the political

sphere, watched it cast a shadow on each of my grandparents, heard harrowing stories about the Holocaust from my maternal grandparents, and witnessed their pain resurface when sharing details of how they'd navigated around death. I'd observed each of them display a remarkable resilience when dealing with adversity, and I needed my family's strength to pulse now in my blood.

My second cousin's wedding was in Central Park that evening and my mom, Debbie, had already arrived from Montreal with her four inseparable siblings. They were the Jewish Brady Bunch, close-knit and wholesome. With the interview, the wedding, and then dinner at Locanda Verde, Robert De Niro's popular Italian restaurant in Tribeca, my schedule was full. But I needed to spend time with Mom before the wedding as well; it had been at least two months since I'd seen her.

I entered the kitchen and pulled open the refrigerator door, squinting as the light met my eyes. After grabbing a bottle of water, I shut the door and returned to the darkness, resting my lower back against the countertop as I twisted the cap off. I took a few sips, returned to my room, and slid between the sheets with an uncomfortable feeling still looming. At some point, I drifted back to sleep.

I was awakened at 7:13 a.m. by my phone vibrating against my right hip and picked it up to find my father, Tarek. I knew my father well, and unless it was necessary, a call at that hour was uncharacteristic of him and indicative of unfavorable news. The last time I'd heard from him at such an hour was nearly six months prior, when he lost his mother, the iconic Egyptian actress Faten Hamama. I shifted into a seated position, rested my head against the headboard, and answered.

"Hey," I said softly.

"Hi. Are you awake?"

"No. Why would I be awake?"

A wave of silence paused the conversation, but I knew there was more. Dad confessed, "I have some bad news."

Sliding my fingers through my cropped hair, I took a deep breath, exhaling as he uttered three grievous words with his factual and stoic demeanor: "Omar is dead."

My eyes widened as an oppressive, numbing sensation swept through my body; I needed to hear it again. "What did you say?"

"It was a heart attack. I don't have much information, but I didn't want you to hear it from someone else."

I rubbed my hand across my face and asked, "Where are you?"

"Paris."

"Are you okay?"

"I have to go and make some more phone calls."

"Okay. Call me back," I added, but he'd already hung up.

I closed my eyes and imagined seeing Omar Sharif— Grandfather—one last time, but he was gone. My chin fell toward my chest as I shook my head in disbelief; the sadness filtered through me. Although we knew the day would come, it came sooner than expected. After a few moments of staring vacantly at the wall in front of me, I sent Mom a short text informing her of Grandfather's passing and dropped the phone back onto my bed. The cause was the same as Grandmother Faten, both at the age of eighty-three. I flung the sheets off my legs, got out of bed, and went into the living room. Shafts of light had permeated the horizontal blinds, softly illuminating the space with increasingly large stripes. I picked up my computer from the coffee table, settled into the cherry-red armchair next to the sofa, and began tapping the keys. "Only God is eternal," I typed in Arabic, and then clicked the share button on Facebook. Grandfather had written a book about his life; it was called *The Eternal Male.*

———

The last time Grandfather and I were together had only been a few months prior, in March of 2015. Celebrated film director Jim Sheridan had reached out to Grandfather, confident he'd be perfect for a role in his new film, *The Secret Scripture.* Until then, I'd merely had a few roles, both film and television, and presented at the Oscars, but as part of the package, Jim offered me a sizable role, too. I loved acting. It was what I wanted to do most, but I hadn't pursued it the way I should have. I was afraid that acting would cast a bigger spotlight on me while I was still in the shadows. I'd already pretended to be someone I wasn't for the majority of my life, and I had no desire to draw increased attention if I wasn't able to be myself.

When I came out, it was surprising that my sexual orientation never became a discussion with Grandfather. He treated me as if nothing had changed in our relationship, and he loved me the same way. Doing a film with Omar Sharif would let the rest of the world know that, too. At thirty years old, working with my grandfather, an iconic actor, would be the highlight of my career.

Given Grandfather's health, Dad was opposed to him taking the role and, without disclosing details, he told Jim, "Omar's not in great shape. I don't know what you'd get out of him." Despite the warning, Jim remained confident he could get what he needed. It wasn't unreasonable for Jim to ask Grandfather to take on another role, because Grandfather was still making films. Only six years prior, he had played an elderly painter with Alzheimer's who becomes a mentor to a young girl in *I Forgot to Tell You*. Full of enthusiasm and connected to his love of acting, Grandfather insisted, "Yes, I'll do it. I want to see Jim."

I felt that part of Grandfather's motivation for doing a film together was his attempt to leave me with something indicative of our bond and special relationship, just as he'd done with my father in *Doctor Zhivago*. We didn't have many photos together, because we enjoyed our time without the distraction of taking them. The limited photographs I have of Grandfather and me are from *Paris Match* or other magazines. I was in favor of doing the film because I knew Grandfather was ailing and I wanted to have something I'd done with him that would live forever.

There were times when I could tell Grandfather was mindful of his declining health, though he didn't always remember what was wrong. Remaining hopeful that he'd be able to shoot on one of his better days, Grandfather selected four consecutive days to travel to Dublin, Ireland, to film on the set of *The Secret Scripture*. By the time we began shooting, what my father had wanted to avoid came to fruition. When anyone approached Grandfather on set, he'd proudly introduce me as his son to one person, and to the next, with the same degree of pride, as his friend. I never corrected him, because he was grasping at whatever came to mind to explain his connection to me. In reality, he didn't know me, either. I followed Grandfather around on set, taking care of him the best I could. Apparently, Jim observed the way I handled him and modified my role, making me Grandfather's caregiver in the film, too.

In one scene, Grandfather was directed to show photographs to the actor Eric Bana and to say, "This was your mother." After

Grandfather leaned forward to examine the photos, he didn't say anything. Instead, his forehead gathered into little lines that pulled closely together, forming deep wrinkles as his eyes narrowed. It appeared as though he were trying to pull an image of the woman or the people in the pictures from his memory but couldn't. When Jim attempted to get Grandfather to deliver the line, he locked eyes with Jim, thumped his index finger on the photo, and insisted, "I don't know any of these people."

It was difficult to watch. The coaching became too much, and Grandfather sat with his shoulders rolled forward in defeat. His dark, sorrowing eyes didn't lie. He was lost—in another world. They continued feeding Grandfather his lines, instructing him to say the words, as if he would snap out of it, but his frustration mounted, and instead he just snapped, "I don't know them! I don't know any of them!"

Grandfather was right; he didn't know the people in the picture or the reason the film team was trying to convince him to say he did. Then it hit me that he wasn't aware he was on set or supposed to be acting at all.

I was proud of my grandfather. He was always so perfect, not a star who was nice to everyone in public but mean to people behind closed doors. He was always in the now, never fake. Grandfather was charming, put together, focused, and eloquent, but on set that day, he was frustrated, confused, lost, agitated, and yelling at people. I was looking at a stranger and a stranger was looking back at me. I tried to be helpful by asking Grandfather to do something that was in the script, but he became angry. He lashed out at me because he believed I was telling him to do it in real life. My face flushed with embarrassment while strangers and bystanders looked on as though *that* was our normal relationship. I was mortified but intent on trying to help Grandfather maintain his dignity by delivering a final product for the film, so I bottled it all up and did what I was there to do.

I assign no blame to Jim and his crew. They were remarkably patient and delicate with Grandfather, doing everything possible to make it work, but in the end, they couldn't accomplish what they needed. They cut Grandfather out of the film, and since the majority of the scenes I'd done were with him, they cut me out, too.

The next morning, I stepped off the elevator to find Grandfather sitting comfortably on a sofa in the opulent lobby of the InterContinental Dublin hotel. He was holding the newspaper open, covering everything except his fingers and the top of his head. My eyes drifted to the familiar face of his French secretary, Catherine. She was sitting across from him, wearing a cream sweater with the brown and black print of a cheetah's face covering the front. As I approached them, I noticed Catherine was occupied with a conversation on the phone. Catherine had been with Grandfather since she was sixteen or seventeen years old, and when our regular driver wasn't available, she'd pick me up from the airport when I traveled to see Grandfather. Like Catherine, and my longtime nanny, Pepita, everyone around Grandfather became family, and they treated me like theirs, which is why I never felt displaced when I was with him. Grandfather had long-standing relationships. Pepita helped raise not only me but also my father.

For as long as I remember, Catherine's smile was as genuine as one could be, and she seemed to carry the same cheerful demeanor wherever she went. Sweeping, soft bangs covered her forehead, and her dirty-blond-and-gray hair cascaded around her neckline with the ends lightly flipped up. Once again, her comforting eyes illuminated beautifully, saying *bonjour* as they always had, before she returned her attention to her call.

Unless Grandfather was working on a film or going to horse races, it would be a rare occasion to see him at that hour. He'd usually wake up at 1:30 or 2:00 in the afternoon, take a bath, and review the racing journals. Committed to a noticeable routine, Grandfather would not have eaten by that time of day. When he'd finally emerge from the confines of his bedroom, cigarette in hand, well-rested, and neatly dressed, we'd watch the end of the Tour de France, then take a leisurely stroll to a local restaurant and have a dinner that would extend past midnight. When I was a young adult, he'd take me to the casino or the horse races, kindly slipping fifty francs into my hand so I could place bets, too. Over time, Grandfather increased the amount, always making certain that when I was with him, we had fun together. He didn't want me sitting at a card table watching him live inside his world as if I were tagging along out of necessity. Grandfather wanted me to be as jovial and engaged as he was, and his friends knew to interact with me in just the same way. Every time he'd lose a hand of cards or an unlikely bet at the racetrack, he'd turn to me and say, "Put your losses in the past and leave them there; tomorrow we win big." Although I never took to gambling and gambling never took to me, those years together were among our best.

That morning, Grandfather appeared to be in good spirits, exuding his distinct brand of innate class and sophistication, causing my grin to broaden as I seated myself next to him on the sofa. A server politely approached me and asked if I'd care for any coffee, tea, or juice. It has never been my preference to drink tea or coffee in the morning, but my eyes darted to the coffee table to see if Grandfather was having his usual. There was a white ceramic teapot, cup, and saucer, and the rest of the morning newspaper spread out in front of him. After observing his disposition on set the day prior, I wanted now, as much as possible, to slip into a world with him that I recognized, if only to have tea. Nodding politely at the server, I asked for another cup.

Dressed in charcoal-gray trousers, a navy jacket, a long-sleeved royal-blue polo, and black shoes, Grandfather looked dapper as always, thanks to Catherine. Carefully studying the expression on his face, it didn't take long before I noticed he wasn't reading the paper at all. Grandfather was looking at the pictures and eagerly turned to show me the faces of football players. He began pointing at each one with childlike laughter escaping his warm grin. That moment was more evidence that, though hard to admit, Grandfather was no longer in this world or even responding to it the way he once had. I glanced at Catherine, and she shrugged as if to say, *This is how he is now.* His soulful brown eyes, mustache, and thick white hair were the same, but a chronic neurodegenerative disease had all but extinguished his internal, intense fire. It was agonizing to realize that his passion for acting, his world-class skills at bridge, his love for crosswords, the long dinners with the most stimulating conversations, and the intellect to do it all had been stolen—without him knowing. Omar Sharif, the Hollywood icon who had received an Oscar nomination and won multiple Golden Globes and a César Award, sat next to me as if it were impossible for him to have accomplished any of it. I conceded that Alzheimer's had come closer day by day, like the tide, until he was completely underwater and had transitioned into an empty vessel.

Our family was always important to Grandfather, but he started to show it a lot more once his health began to falter. Maybe he was afraid he hadn't done enough, but I think it was that he'd forgotten.

I'd been aware of his diagnosis and had watched the progression of nearly every stage for almost ten years. It was painful. Once Grandfather reached late-stage Alzheimer's, any time he seemed to understand something, the disease surfaced and swallowed his thoughts as quickly as it had his memories. Entering Grandfather's world and *fully* understanding what he saw, felt, and remembered was impossible, but from the outside, I watched Grandfather lose a lifetime.

In the first few years, Grandfather's decline was slow and appeared to be part of the natural aging process. By the second stage, our relationship changed and I became more of a caregiver when we were together. Each adjustment coincided with the progression of the disease, and I made them without letting him know I was doing it. I never wanted to embarrass Grandfather. He was too proud.

For over forty years, when Grandfather was in France, he frequently dined at Chez Miocque, a restaurant owned by a family friend in the seaside resort of Deauville near the Casino Barrière. Photographs of celebrities, including Grandfather, who had dined there covered the walls and ceilings of the establishment. We never looked at a menu; we knew it by heart. We'd always start by ordering wine and several of the appetizers for everyone to share and proceed with one course after another. One evening, Grandfather and I were dining alone, and dinner presented a different narrative. When it was time for the main course, the server asked Grandfather what he was having, and Grandfather looked at me as if he didn't know how to respond. He needed help communicating what he wanted. I suggested a variety of items he typically selected, pretending to decide for myself.

"The *sole meunière* sounds good. I remember how much you enjoyed that last time," I told him. "And the *escalopes de veau* is always delicious." I sighed expressively, entertaining the idea of two of his favorites, hoping one of them would appeal to him.

Grandfather didn't reply to the server. Instead, he turned to me and asked, "So, what are you having?"

When I told him, his eyes lit up and he smiled triumphantly. He looked up at the server and confidently exclaimed, "I'll have the same."

Grandfather had dined all around the world and had quite a discerning palate, but when the server returned to see how everything was, instead of replying confidently, he glanced at me, checking for validation, and questioned, "It's good?" When I smiled and nodded in agreement, he answered again with more assurance and cheer, "*Merveilleux*!" I realized Grandfather couldn't recall what was on the menu, nor did he know exactly what he was eating. From that point on, as soon as I detected a lapse in memory or difficulty with his decision-making or communication, I'd make subtle decisions on his behalf, without him knowing it.

The little modifications were constant, and over time, they became more significant. Whenever we went out to dinner, the horse races, or anywhere else, I'd make slight adjustments to his appearance. I'd brush light dandruff off his shoulders before we'd get out of the car to go into a restaurant, adjust his tie, recommend something he would normally have chosen on his own, and guide him in the direction we were heading when he seemed lost. I was careful not to do anything in a condescending or patronizing way. I simply managed the little things that would not have escaped Omar Sharif.

Over the next six or seven years, Grandfather became more withdrawn and increasingly agitated due to his inability to remember some of his most cherished memories. They were the fabulous stories I'd heard him tell at the dinner table for decades, keeping everyone completely captivated. Grandfather didn't recite stories; he had mastered the art of recreating the color, characters, and clarity as if he were there once again. As his recollections melted together, he told the same stories out of chronological order. Before anyone noticed, I'd ask a question to redirect or interrupt his recounting, and he'd seldom remember to go back to it. If something upset Grandfather, I'd bring up memories that took him to a happier place, and somehow, he'd regain his composure. They were usually stories about Barbra Streisand or Peter O'Toole. My father and Catherine were the only other people I knew who could discreetly guide Grandfather in a better direction without him knowing, leaving his dignity intact.

Eventually, stories he told that were familiar to us, or even to the public, didn't make sense. Grandfather wasn't lying about the stories he innocently attempted to share—the disease was in the process of eradicating his memory. It began erasing one colorful line at a time, advancing to paragraphs, and then chapters of his life. Fragmented memories left by the disease were what Grandfather had to work with, and whatever he said was what he believed happened. It seemed that Grandfather was deteriorating faster than time, and one day, his personality changed to someone I no longer knew.

Just two years before our time in Dublin, Grandfather and I were at Fouquet's, a crowded restaurant in Paris, enjoying our time together over dinner. He appeared to be in good spirits, laughing as he recounted pieces of familiar stories. This never bothered me, because I could fill in the gaps. This was as close as Grandfather came to the way he used to be, and I was grateful for that time with him. I closed my eyes to savor the moment.

"Omar. Are you okay?" Grandfather asked. I opened my eyes to find him looking at me curiously.

"Yes, I'm fine."

"Then, what? What is it?"

"I'm just happy to be spending time with you," I replied.

His dismissive laughter was interwoven with the beginning of a story, followed by another. Somehow, I brought up his love for horses, reminding him of the time he'd taken me to a horse auction in Deauville. Grandfather placed a forkful of salad in his mouth and leaned back in his chair, listening attentively as if it were the first time he'd heard of it.

Deauville is renowned in the horse-racing world for its races and for its thoroughbred auctions. The auction I had attended was filled with people from around the world, but the excitement had come from being with Grandfather. I loved watching people approach him and studying his interactions, and I could tell that his focus never wavered from the impressive collection of horses. Before the auction, the horses were taken on the round, where potential buyers closely scrutinized their movements, taking notes, and chatting amongst themselves. I stood next to Grandfather, admiring one thoroughbred with a dark chestnut coat and a slightly lighter mane. Her muscles rolled beneath her glossy coat each time she walked past, and she turned her head to stare directly at me with her dark brown eyes. I mentioned this to Grandfather, and he dismissed it with his signature laughter. When the bidding started, we went inside, but there weren't any available seats. While the auctioneer rambled on, inaudible bidding went as high as two million euros that afternoon. The dark chestnut horse that kept eyeing me went for 14,000 euros and had a new home. While leaving the auction, Grandfather was handed a yellow slip, and I was shocked to learn that he had secretly purchased her for me. We spent the following two days coming up with names and decided to call her Dinner Time. For our favorite pastime together.

My horse didn't seem like the best investment, because she had a distinctive walk that resembled a limp; nevertheless, she won several group races and was decidedly good for breeding. Later, she sold for nearly half a million euros.

"Do you remember that?" I asked Grandfather.

He laughed and nodded his head affirmatively.

"You bought me my first horse, and then my first car with some of the earnings."

"Yes. And Catherine—no, Pepita—she took you to riding lessons—and to polo," he added.

"Yes, she did," I replied, pleased that he remembered. I assured him that my summers in the north of France were always the best.

An hour into dinner, Grandfather stopped talking and pushed his plate away as though the food were awful.

"Is something wrong?" I asked.

Grandfather didn't respond. Instead, he dabbed his mouth with the napkin and sat back in his chair, shifting his face to a meditative expression. I glanced around the dining room to assess the size of our audience and cringed. Every table was seated, the noise was at a minimum and the ambient music playing in the background was delicate. Grandfather bit down slightly on one side of his bottom lip, fixing me with cold, piercing dark eyes. Responding to the abrupt change in his mood, I became uncomfortable and mentally prepared for whatever was about to transpire. I placed my knife and fork together on the right edge of my plate, certain that the course was my last; his anger was swift.

"Do you know what's wrong with you?" he stated resolutely, sounding as though he did.

"No," I answered.

"You're not handsome," he began. I lowered my head and swallowed hard. He'd never said anything like that before. "And you are not talented! You aren't," he said, shrugging apathetically. "You want to be something, but you are never going to be anything like I was because you will always be a failure! And you—you are never going to be anything like me," he scoffed.

His brutal wrath echoed throughout the dining room, garnering attention from complete strangers who turned sharply toward us. I didn't defend myself, because I never thought there would or could be another Omar Sharif, but in this moment, he wasn't Omar either, and the people around us looking at him with apprehension didn't know that. He wasn't saying those things because he was jealous of me building a career; he was suffering from his own decline. My eyes glazed over. I remained frozen in that space, traumatized by his attack while he blasted me with a barrage of cutting insults. I didn't think he could get any louder, but somehow he managed it with each one. Both embarrassed and saddened by his unmanageable behavior, I knew the best thing for me to do was to sit quietly and take it. Moving his hands expressively as he spoke, Grandfather knocked over a glass, spilling red wine across the crisp, white tablecloth. More people stared and whispered, but he didn't appear to notice or care. From the corner of my eye, I saw an older gentleman with a stern look get up and head toward us. As we made eye contact, I slowly shook my head for him not to intervene. He'd only make it worse. Another middle-aged woman came from behind me, placed her hand on my shoulder and said in French, "Why do you put up with that? Why don't you get up and walk away?" She shook her head disapprovingly at Grandfather, expecting him to be shamefaced, but he wasn't. "Come with me," she insisted, reaching for my hand.

Glancing up at her, I replied in a whisper, "It's okay. We just have to get through this." She patted my shoulder and hesitantly walked away.

I sat, fidgeting with the cloth napkin on my lap until Grandfather ran out of insults and anger. Although he had plenty to say, he didn't utter a single word about me being gay or my letter published in *The Advocate* just six months prior.

Eventually, Grandfather realized what he was doing, and the tide washed back out, signaling it was time to leave. I didn't want anyone to see that his eyes welled with tears or to hear him sobbing. When we left the restaurant, he started hitting himself in the head and pulling at his shirt over his heart, crying, "I don't know why I do this! I don't know why I hurt the people I love the most!"

That evening, complete strangers watched as if I had the most abusive grandfather, but I didn't. I was just getting to know *this* man.

I handled Grandfather the best way I knew how, but it was terrible to see my father on the receiving end. There were many occasions that Grandfather did the same thing to Dad, and just as I had, he'd sit there and take it. We loved him. Regardless of how he treated us in those moments, we'd never leave him alone in that world or this one. He needed us. He was our family and we wanted to take care of him, just as he had cared for us.

When I read what the press had written about my grandfather's brushes with the law and his unfavorable behavior in public, it hurt. We knew he had Alzheimer's—they didn't. The press reported what they heard or thought they were witnessing, but it wasn't actually what had transpired. Over the years, Alzheimer's took nearly everything from Grandfather; however, his ability to speak Arabic, English, French, Spanish, Italian, and other languages fluently lasted to the end. I could tell when Grandfather didn't know what people were talking about, but with his signature smile, he'd still speak whatever language was in the air.

In Grandfather's final year, the only thing in control was time, and it worked intimately with Alzheimer's to remove the memories of his life. Always adorning his wrist was his favorite Cartier watch with a small white face, a gold trim, and a black leather band. Near the end, he even believed that the watch had mystical powers. He'd tap on the face and say, "This watch is magic." Subconsciously, he was probably communicating that his time was running out.

I found it remarkable that Grandfather had a few stories from decades past that even Alzheimer's couldn't extinguish. We must all have hidden treasures in our minds that nothing or no one can steal. What Omar Sharif fought to preserve must have been from the absolute best part of his life. In the end, Alzheimer's relegated one of the most famous people in the world to an unknown landscape, lost in time and space, isolated to scraps of memories and few friends.

Throughout the years, Grandfather and I spent a great deal of time together. We rarely took pictures, but before I left him in Dublin, I needed to have one more memory in hand. When I asked Grandfather to take a photo with me, his unpretentious look of surprise was unforgettable. As a child, I'd sit at the dinner table and he'd teasingly make faces at me. It was part of our playful exchange. That morning, he put his hands up like two claws and made one of those silly faces. Without hesitation, I did the same. Catherine quickly captured on my phone what would be my last moment with Grandfather.

I embraced my grandfather, whom I always called Omar, with my soul and kissed him on both of his whiskered cheeks before watching him walk away. It was reminiscent of the last scene in *Funny Girl* when Grandfather's character, Nick Arnstein, stood in the dressing room with Barbra Streisand's character, Fanny Brice, seated at a vanity mirror. He was charming, gallant, and the air of sophistication about him remained intact even though he was aware he was about to go to jail. He kissed Barbra goodbye and walked out of the dressing room. I couldn't help but acknowledge the pain in Barbra's vibrant blue eyes. As Grandfather left, I felt a lot like that, too. He walked out just as dignified as he walked in, only this time, I was left, broken, in the chair.

That morning, Grandfather returned to Egypt, and I went back to my apartment in New York. The reported heart attack wasn't the cause of my grandfather's death; Alzheimer's had ravaged him for years until there was nothing left.

———

I heard my phone vibrating from the bedroom and knew it was Mom calling in response to my text. I put the computer back on the coffee table and returned to the phone lying on my bed. Expecting to be bombarded with a series of questions I wasn't prepared to answer, I picked up, reiterated my text to her, and quickly got off the phone before heading into the bathroom to brush my teeth and shower. I didn't know how to process Grandfather's passing, so I internalized the grief and opted to move forward with my day. Forty-five minutes later, I was dressed and walking out the door, in conversation with a family member in Egypt.

I boarded a crowded subway train headed to the Flatiron District, deliberating whether I should take the risk and return to Egypt for Grandfather's funeral. As the rhythmic sound and movement of the train began, I stared out the window, as if I were in a catatonic state or my mind had shut down, but it hadn't. I had plunged deeper into thought. Time was crucial, and I was aware that by Muslim custom, Grandfather would be buried before sundown that day, even if relatives couldn't make it in time for the funeral. At the latest, it would take place before sundown the following day. If I didn't figure things out quickly, I wouldn't make it in time.

I had close friends in Morocco who called that morning, offering to help me acquire diplomatic immunity so I could return home, but it wasn't that simple. There was a great deal to consider, such as the sobering conversations I'd had with my family in Egypt. They didn't shy away from voicing their opinions, and one in particular explicitly communicated that the idea was ill-advised. Dad was in a bad state, and she thought I might risk being thrown in jail as soon as I got off the plane. "I don't want to tell you not to come home, but think about your father's health. Let's not cause him added stress," she warned.

I had heard what happened to people imprisoned in Egypt, especially people like me. I didn't have to imagine anything, because I knew the threat was real. I'd already received thousands of them. I remembered my Uncle Simon telling me that it had taken Grandfather Omar's appeal to stop those threatening my life or well-being. He had pleaded with them not to harm me for coming out. He didn't want them to take his grandson's life for finally having the courage to live openly and authentically. Of the many things I knew about Grandfather, one was that he stood for both tolerance and acceptance, and he didn't back down from that position nor change his opinion of me. I hung up the phone, understanding the possibility of jail was a viable threat, due to the actions I had taken over three years prior—when I chose to stop being invisible and share my truth.

I couldn't forget the images of young Egyptians from different religious and socioeconomic backgrounds crowded in Tahrir Square, in what were to be nonviolent demonstrations targeting the Mubarak government over legal and political matters. I had heard accounts from people who were punched in the head, kicked, and stabbed by competing camps of supporters. I knew what Egyptian society could do to anyone who wasn't what they wanted them to be. The demand for change had caused violent clashes with police that killed over eight hundred people and wounded a reported six thousand plus in the Egyptian revolution of 2011. Cairo had become a war zone because there could be no understanding or compromise. That same hate in Egypt was strong enough to wound me, too, because I'd brought awareness to something they wanted to keep out of the light of existence, hidden from the rest of the world.

As if rehearsed, when the subway train jolted to a stop, commuters crammed tightly together and quickly exited while others impatiently waited on the platform to get on. I climbed the stairs out of the tunnel, leaving the rail sounds, darkness, and stale air behind as I continued down West 28th Street across Sixth Avenue. I arrived at my destination early, feeling lost, so I took a moment to regroup before entering the building.

I went to the seventeenth floor and checked in. Minutes later, the gentlemen interviewing me came out into the lobby and shook my hand as he introduced himself. Kevin's even blend of tapered black and gray hair made him look distinguished. His eyes were gentle, as though he had long ago discovered the secret to maintaining internal peace and happiness. He escorted me into his office and motioned for me to have a seat in the chair in front of his neatly organized desk. Before delving into my background and proposal, Kevin's eyes traveled from my suit to my posture and back to my eyes, indicating he was studying me or trying to determine if I was in the right mental state for the interview. It was apparent that he'd already heard the news when he asked, "How are you doing?"

"Unsure," I admitted. "My grandfather passed this morning."

"With great sadness, our receptionist made me aware of his passing a half hour ago. Please accept my deepest condolences."

"Thank you," I replied faintly.

"What are you doing here?" he asked, sympathetically.

I had thought it was best to go to the interview, as I didn't want to be alone. I didn't give a verbal response. I shrugged, discreetly wiped away a tear that was beginning to form in my left eye and repositioned myself, making it clear to Kevin that I was prepared to discuss the opportunity.

Approximately an hour later, I had completed the interview and felt confident I would receive the grant. Kevin walked me out, shook my hand, and said he'd be in touch. When I exited the elevator in the lobby, I pulled out my phone and sent Mom a text to see where she was. When she replied, I headed over to Macy's, only a few blocks away, to meet up with her and her sister, Anne.

———

With her blond hair pulled back off her shoulders and fashionably dressed in white Lululemon athleisure wear, Mom hugged me as though she hadn't seen me in years. Wearing a similar outfit in black, with her strawberry-blond hair glistening in the sun, Anne followed suit. They looked beautiful and greeted me with the love and warmth I'd always known.

Mom's cinnamon-colored eyes raked over me as she asked, "How are you?"

"I'm okay," I lied. I didn't want Mom worrying about me any more than she already was, but I knew she didn't believe me; her reply was a weak smile.

"I don't want to go to the wedding," I confessed.

"You don't have to," she replied. Anne ran her hand soothingly across my back.

Mom and I were close, and by this point, she knew me well. She didn't want me to be alone and thought keeping me busy would take my mind off Grandfather, so she invited me to join them. I rarely went shopping, because I didn't enjoy it. I agreed to go because I believed Mom might be right, but she wasn't. Following them around from one place to another proved to be more stressful than I'd thought. I tried to make the best of it, looking at men's underwear, shoes, distressed jeans, and labels on garments that caught my eye, but I felt uncomfortable. Although I was hovering close to Mom and Anne, I wasn't really reacting to anything they said or showed me; I was just grateful that they were in New York and that I wasn't alone.

Meanwhile, my phone seemed to vibrate every five seconds, indicating an incoming message from family, friends, Twitter, or Facebook. My manager called, informing me about the press inquiries she was receiving and wanting to know how to handle them. As soon as I hung up, I received a call from my close friend Rich, a publicist. He asked if I wanted him to help prepare a statement on behalf of my family. I'd already received thousands of messages offering condolences from people all over the world, so I said, "Yes. Can you please just thank everyone for the outpouring of support?"

One phone call after another required my attention, and I couldn't think, distracted by weaving between dense groups of people, some struggling with more shopping bags than they could manage. In one store, the sales staff interrupted my calls continuously to show me something they thought was essential to have in my wardrobe, and I couldn't take any more. The worst part was that everything was a distraction from what I needed to feel, and I couldn't feel anything. I was no longer in the moment, experiencing it. It was like being a wedding planner rather than the bride or groom. I couldn't be a mourner, because I was organizing the mourning on this side of the world. Every so often, Mom turned around, just to look at me. It was her way of ensuring that I was okay while calls continued. The press was eager for information about Grandfather's life and death, but for the most part, they were more interested in a statement of validation that I loved him than in my desire to give thanks for the outpouring of support, as if I had some ugly gossip to spread. I was so busy trying to give other people what they needed that I neglected myself. When Rich called back, I wandered around a boutique scheduling interviews with him, while Mom and Anne continued trying to get me to look at clothing.

Being in public wasn't helping. My heart palpitations grew heavy and perspiration covered my body. I could hardly breathe. I stepped outside to find clusters of people rushing about the cobblestone streets of Soho covered with cars. As we walked away from one small boutique, a young Middle Eastern man in his early twenties walked up and politely asked me to take a photo with him. Afterward, he thanked me and began to walk away, then spun around and asked, "Hey, didn't your grandfather pass today?" Warmth flushed across my face and my eyes shifted shamefully to the little circular glass bulbs beneath my feet as I nodded. I should have trusted my judgment because the last place I wanted to be was needlessly out in public that Friday morning. Flattened by a massive wave of guilt, I told Mom, "I have to get out of here; this isn't right. I'll see you at the wedding." Without further explanation, I slipped through the crowds of people as though I had evaporated into the air. I wasn't looking forward to going to a wedding, smiling, and pretending to be okay when I wasn't, but I felt it was the right thing to do. I just had to convince myself I could follow through. I went home and completely shut down so I could make it through the long evening ahead.

———

The wedding was in Central Park, near a large pond with a half-dozen rowboats, some drifting aimlessly like me. The trees and lush grass were even more vibrant against the colorful flowers in bloom, adding to the beauty of the surroundings. To combat the heat, the guys were dressed in lightweight or linen suits, and the ladies wore sleeveless or short-sleeved, free-flowing dresses. The night before, I'd put aside a linen suit, but chose a black suit before the wedding instead. I was mourning. I didn't want to be seen in a salmon-colored suit, so I stood in the park, in the absurd heat and humidity, looking awkward and out of place. I was happy for my cousin, but I really needed a quiet place and time to grieve. Instead, that day was about managing expectations. Mom and my aunts and uncles had driven from Canada for the wedding, and I felt an obligation to spend time with them, not off somewhere alone.

After the ceremony, people lined up to congratulate and offer well-wishes to the newlyweds in one breath and, in the next, turned to me and extended heartfelt condolences with the opposite expression. The dinner reception was pleasant, and had it not been for Grandfather's passing, it would have been perfect. My eyes casually drifted around the table to our family and friends toasting, laughing, and having the most delightful time. Of all the wonderful things Grandfather and I had done together, dinners happened to be our favorite. There wasn't one favorite in particular; we loved every one. As I was typically the only child at the table, all Grandfather's friends would become my friends. We'd enjoy the most delicious foods and drink good wine while generating interesting, intoxicating, and intellectual discussions about everything imaginable. Sometimes he'd engage his friends with a game of charades. Grandfather had been a master at keeping everyone drawn into the conversation. He would jump from one language to another, effortlessly managing the attention of his guests. My fluency in six languages allowed me to stay involved in their exchanges and laugh right along with them.

Returning from my reverie, I weakly stood up, trying not to draw attention to myself, and abandoned the celebration at our dinner table, making my way over to the ornate bar in the main dining room. Mom's older brother Holden followed closely behind. We seated ourselves at the bar and quickly downed four shots of tequila each. After placing my fourth shot glass on the bar, I checked the time, said goodbye to Holden, and disappeared through the doors.

Instead of hailing a cab, I decided to walk home, hoping the night air might relieve some of the pain. In that crowded restaurant, surrounded by love, I'd never felt so empty. A part of me was missing. The adage goes that when an old relative dies, they can haunt you, but in this case my grandfather's absence was haunting. For thirty years, the only thing I successfully knew how to be was his grandson. He was always with me, in the corner of the room, behind the door; people saw him standing next to me even if he was on the other side of the world. As Omar Sharif's grandson, bearer of the same name, so much of my identity belonged to him. Now, he was gone, and I was alone. For once, I was just myself, and it was terrifying.

———

By the time I arrived at my apartment, Grandfather's funeral was about to begin in Cairo. When I found a live stream, I turned up the volume, sat up straight in front of my computer as if I were in attendance, and took everything in just as I had done with Grandmother Faten. At the time, I had to watch her funeral on YouTube like an outsider—it was depressing. I couldn't help but feel that Egypt was punishing me once again.

People are quick to say *be yourself*, as if that's easy to do. *Be proud of who you are*, they say, as if the world is ready for that. *Tell the truth—* but when I did, after years of hiding in fear, I was banished from my home in Egypt—forced into exile for being myself. The ramifications were tremendous, and because of them, the only way I'd be able to say my final goodbye to Grandfather was through a flat, impersonal screen from the confines of my small New York City apartment.

When they entered the mosque, carrying the coffin past the line of mourners and throngs of international press, all I could do was imagine being there. When the camera panned over the horizontal line of family and friends inside the mosque, the grief-stricken expressions on the faces of my father and my little brother, Karem, broke my heart. Although Karem and I had different mothers and a sixteen-year age difference between us, we were extremely close. I wanted to be there to pay my last respects, and for Dad, but I should have been there for Karem, too. I leaned in toward the computer screen when the camera zoomed in on my father's face. It was frail; he had never looked older than he did that day. I could only imagine what losing both parents within six months had done to him. Seeing my dad made me worry about him, the same way he always worried about me. But I couldn't be there to help him through this or take care of him. I couldn't go home. Egypt no longer wanted me, so I kissed my finger and touched the screen.

After the funeral at the Hussein Tantawi Mosque, Grandfather's coffin, draped with the Egyptian flag and a black shroud, was rushed into the back of a car and driven off. I closed my computer and exhaled.

I spent the rest of the early morning in silence. I picked up my phone and began reading and responding to the incalculable messages of sympathy sent through text and social media channels. When the heaviness became too much, I took a long, hot shower, hoping the pelting streams of warmth would strip off the layers of pain and wash them away. But when I stepped out of the shower, the pain had increased and the emptiness inside of me was weakening. There were no more distractions to the day, and I could feel everything. I went into my room and collapsed onto my bed, held captive by more thoughts of what had been.

2

Worlds Apart

The next morning, I took the time to manage what I was feeling. After responding to a handful of calls, including one from Rich, I finished a bottle of coconut water and headed to the gym a few blocks away. The press wasn't finished, and I had to prepare for what lay ahead. If journalists were going to ask questions, I wanted to make sure they had the right answers. The reported accounts of Grandfather's legacy needed to be accurate, which is why I accepted every request for an interview that my publicist received. Within a few days, I had significant press opportunities. One of them called for international travel, so I boarded an overnight flight to do a live, sit-down interview in Arabic on a popular youth-oriented talk show. Televised on DW's Arabic channel, the interview would be my first exclusive in the region since coming out. Going to Egypt wasn't a viable option, so the interview with Jaafar Abdul Karim on *Shababtalk*, scheduled to be forty-five minutes long, was held at their Berlin studio. When I arrived at the studio, it dawned on me that the interview might be a setup, and I became uneasy. So-called "gotcha" journalism is common in the Arab world. I hadn't done an Arabic interview about coming out, a taboo subject in the Middle East, because I couldn't control the substance or tone of questioning once we went live. To protect myself, I advised the producers that if they asked anything inappropriate, I would sabotage the live interview.

The interview was going well, but when Jaafar asked about Grandfather's funeral, he repeatedly questioned my absence. I didn't want to address it because I couldn't go home, and it wasn't something I wanted to admit. I've always tried to remain optimistic—*one day I will go home.* If I explained why, the interview would have a negative tone. I tried talking around the question, but Jaafar didn't stop, so I removed my earpiece and said, "I'm having some trouble with the audio." I sat in silence until he moved on to a question that I was more comfortable answering. When the interview was over, I had accomplished what I went there to do: paid tribute and respect to my grandparents' lives and legacy, showcased our unbreakable family bond and loving relationships, and shared my full and authentic self as a mourning grandchild, regardless of whether I was gay or straight. It's since been estimated that some four million people watched the show live, and many regard it as the first time people in the region heard directly from an openly LGBTQ person, and it was certainly the first from someone they watched grow up from a young age who would appeal to their hearts and minds.

Feeling emotionally drained, I boarded the flight home. Speaking about Grandfather and Faten reminded me that I was still vulnerable to the pain of losing them. While I was buckled up in my seat, patiently waiting for the plane to take off, a flight attendant came over and said, "My name is Sami. I'm sorry about your grandfather."

"Thank you. I appreciate that."

"And, Mr. Sharif," he began.

"Yes?" I replied.

"I admire you as a person. You changed my life—in a good way."

"Really?"

"I live in Berlin because you gave me the courage to find *my* freedom."

"Now that you've found it, stay true and embrace it," I told him.

An announcement that the plane was prepared for takeoff interrupted our conversation.

"I will," he said, snapping overhead compartments closed as he hurried down the aisle.

I thought about how different my life had been in the States compared to my life in Egypt. I had great friends and went to good parties, as I had in Egypt, but in New York, I lived the way I'd always wanted to—openly, authentically, and happily. I found it incomprehensible that people would not want that for everyone.

While living in New York over the previous two years, I had become part of the movement fighting for LGBTQ equality in the United States and across the globe. I did news interviews regularly and spoke at events for GLAAD while traveling extensively around the States, laying the groundwork in hopes that soon the Supreme Court would declare same-sex marriage legal across the land. When it happened in 2015, I remained hopeful that Egypt, along with the rest of the world, might one day embrace acceptance, too. In a sense, the LGBTQ community gave me the same platform that Hollywood had given Grandfather decades before. If I could use this platform to change one flight attendant's life, maybe it was all worth it. I turned off my reading light, tucked the pillow behind my head, and closed my eyes. Shortly after the plane's rapid ascent, I pushed the button to recline my seat and fell into the first restful sleep I'd had in weeks.

———

The questions Jaafar Abdul Karim asked in Berlin brought to mind how disparate the cultures, religions, and continents that I navigated between actually were. Traditional cuisine, in both worlds, is an example of cultural identity that we cling to. The time we spent as a family enjoying meals kept us connected not only to our culture but to each other. When I visited family in Cairo, my Grandmother Faten would open the front door and kiss both my cheeks, as the welcoming aroma of my favorite meals, like *molokhia* or *bamya*, wafted out from behind her. Although she had an entire staff to take care of us, she enjoyed doing many of those traditional things herself.

As long as I can remember, I felt that I lived in two different worlds. My father's side of the family in Egypt was one, and my mother's in Canada was another. As a child, when I understood that I was different and realized that difference was viewed negatively, I created my own internal world out of necessity rather than choice. My world was convoluted, and I couldn't allow anyone in it for most of my life.

My name was the reason I appeared privileged, but the truth is that I had to fight for more than anyone could imagine. Regardless of the destination, along every step of the way was a crisis teaching me how to be a fighter and, ultimately, a survivor.

———

As Grandfather tells the story, it was somewhat by accident that he facilitated the introduction of my parents to one another. He was staying at the Ritz-Carlton while making a film in Montreal. Dining alone was never his preference, so when my mother, Debbie, took up the dare of a friend to introduce herself at a bar one evening, Omar responded, "My son is coming to visit me tomorrow. If you don't have any plans, would you like to bring some of your friends and join us for dinner?"

Mom replied, "Yes. I have a friend. I'll bring her."

When Dad arrived, Grandfather told him, "I invited two ladies for dinner, one blond and one brunette."

Dad was immediately drawn to the blond over dinner, which was Mom. They instantly hit it off and spent the rest of the night dancing at Club 1234 on Rue de la Montagne.

Although Mom was Jewish and Dad Muslim, they married and were together for three years, only to divorce when I was nine months old. Their divorce was unpleasant and Mom had significant health issues, but she did everything she could for me. My father remained in Montreal to be near me every second weekend and on holidays, keeping to his custody agreement.

———

For the first few years after the divorce, my mother and I lived intermittently with her parents, Bubbie and Zadie. I was just four years old when Bubbie began sharing stories of the Holocaust and her childhood in Poland, smuggling food into the Warsaw Ghetto, the concentration camps and death marches, giving the most graphic descriptions about the plight and demise of her entire family. When

Bubbie spoke of the Nazis, I couldn't process who they were, so I imagined them as kidnappers who'd kick down our door, take us away, and kill us the way they did the Jews in Europe. I didn't understand that the Holocaust was over, either; the only ending to the Holocaust in the stories was marked by death, destruction, and despair. It was then that I surmised that shadows and darkness hid something terrible. Before bed, I'd go from one room to another checking to see if my grandparents had locked the windows. I'd secure each one, placing a piece of wood from a broomstick handle inside the frame to prevent the Nazis from opening the windows. The slightest noise at night made me jump out of bed, race down the hall to Bubbie and Zadie's bedroom, and wedge myself securely between them. Like superheroes, they had beat the Nazis to survive, so surely they could protect me. I inherited that trauma as a third-generation Holocaust survivor, and I was afraid to sleep alone until I was nine.

Bubbie's sister's last words to her during the selection process at the gates of the Majdanek concentration camp were, "Survive. Remember. Do everything you can to survive so you can tell the world what happened to us." Bubbie had managed to do just that. She told the truth, hoping it would empower us. Though Bubbie had experienced the worst of humanity and remembered every frightening detail of her persecution, she continued to see the best in everyone. She regularly took complete strangers off the street and into her home to feed and shelter them, without judgment. The tattoo of the number 48378 branded along with a little upside-down triangle on her forearm in Auschwitz didn't change her. Bubbie displayed compassion in the most beautiful ways, convincing me that it was her lifelong mission to help others and save lives any way she could. In time, it became evident that she was trying to pass along the good others had done for her, the little acts of kindness that helped her survive where so many others perished. Bubbie's capacity to forgive after all that was taken from her made her my heroine.

Zadie saw through a different lens. He had watched as the Nazis dragged his family from their home and boarded them on a train to Treblinka, where they were immediately exterminated in the crematorium. Neighbors had to forcibly hold him back from trying to join them. Unlike Bubbie, the hate that was shown to Zadie and his family never left him. He questioned everything and trusted no one outside our family. Bubbie and Zadie responded differently to that same tragedy, but what they had in common was their love and devotion to family. They kept us close by having us all come together multiple times every week to eat and discuss whatever was going on in our lives.

I didn't know it then, but their stories would have a tremendous influence on me. Bubbie's choice to see the best in humanity became my measure for people. If my grandmother could forgive the Germans, I could forgive, too. I chose to see humanity as good—and when it wasn't, I'd believe it would get better.

———

Divorced families typically have some degree of conflict, and we had ours. My parents were still going to court for custody battles to fight over minute details that had somehow become significant. There seemed to be conflict on every level, both external and internal, on one side or the other. It impacted my childhood, as I didn't spend my time hanging out with friends or playing ball in Canada during vacations and holidays. By the age of six, I was taking transatlantic flights alone with a sign hanging around my neck so the flight attendants could hand me off at each airport without incident. My summer vacations were allocated for time with Grandmother Faten in Egypt. Sometimes, we'd travel on her yacht in the Red Sea or to one of her homes in Agami along the Mediterranean shore. There I'd wake up to the sweet smell of fresh-cut mango and blossoming fig trees and lounge under the gazebo with my friends or swim in her kidney-shaped pool. I spent the last two weeks of my vacation with Grandfather Omar. At some point, Dad would join me for ten days before returning to Canada for work. When a vacation or holiday came to an end, the sign went back around my neck, and I flew home to Mom.

My parents were from different worlds, nationalities, religions, backgrounds, upbringings, and socioeconomic groups, and I was the piece of rope in the middle. I realized early that if I were going to live happily, I couldn't allow them to pull on me in either direction. I got both sides to stop tugging by loving them equally and blending seamlessly—and invisibly—into each of their worlds.

I spent the first twelve years of my life living in Montreal, shuffling between my parents. When Dad realized the opportunities to work in Egypt were better, he left Montreal. I knew my father didn't want to leave me, so his absence didn't threaten our bond. It was no longer convenient for Dad to take me to see two movies at a time, play board games for hours, ride rollercoasters with me at La Ronde—the amusement park in Montreal—or let me fall asleep at his flat watching music videos, but he stayed involved in my life. Change really was constant, and since it happened from a young age, I adapted and grew up in both worlds, with both sets of rules, customs, traditions, and cultures. It developed into something quite natural for me, although this wasn't so for my parents.

I was an obedient child, so discipline wasn't an issue; I didn't get in trouble. I listened more than anything, became a quick study, and determined what the advantages and disadvantages were to life in each world. It was *A Tale of Two Cities*: "It was the best of times, it was the worst of times."

Being raised by a single mother taught me to be independent, and how to survive, make decisions, and be accountable. When Mom and I moved into our comfortable two-bedroom apartment, if I wasn't with Dad, Bubbie and Zadie took care of me to give Mom a break. Mom worked in advertising, and after work, she went to the gym or the social club to hang out with friends. When I was in elementary school, we maintained a standard routine. I either rode the school bus home or walked to my aunt Anne's home, where I had dinner and hung out with my cousins, Jessica, Michael, and Zoe, until Mom picked me up at eight. At home, I'd sit in the den or the living room and do my homework. If I needed any help, Mom would sit down and work with me until it was done. Most weekends, and occasionally during the week, I spent time with Bubbie and Zadie at their duplex. If we weren't gardening in the backyard, they'd rent movies and we'd nestle together comfortably on the sofa watching one after another.

I've always had the constant attention of my family. While Aunt Anne offered comfort and understanding, Aunt Evelyn tendered support, honest opinions, and tough love. There was no sugar coating, but the love in the center was sweet. When I was young, Evelyn took her children, Lisa and Mitchell, to Disney World. She knew Mom couldn't afford to take me, so she packed my things and took me along with them. Evelyn wanted me to have the same experiences as her children. She loved museums, art, and culture. As I grew older, they captured my attention, too, and we had that in common. Whenever I had a problem, she was my sounding board. She didn't agree with everything I did or how I did it after coming out—but she made her shoulder available anytime I needed it. When I was younger, Evelyn, like her siblings, was instrumental in taking care of Mom, and when I fell in a hole, she likewise supported me, emotionally and financially.

Somehow, Uncle Holden knew that I needed attention and guidance, and he always went above and beyond in treating me like a son. He taught me to skate and play hockey, becoming the reason I did well in sports. I didn't have many friends, but I had my uncle Holden. When the Montreal Canadiens won the Stanley Cup in 1993, Holden showed up at my school and signed me out early. Making me promise not to tell my parents, he took me to the Stanley Cup parade downtown, outside the old Forum. I'd never seen so many people pouring into the streets. When the crowd became too dense for me to see the parade, Uncle Holden lifted me up, sat me on his shoulders, and said, "You're witnessing history. This might not happen again for a very long time." The Canadiens were part of our family tradition, and it was exciting to watch their games or listen to them on the radio with Zadie, my uncles, Holden and Simon, and my cousins. It made us feel more Canadian. Hockey is how my family assimilated.

My mom was a young mother, and she hadn't finished university, but she did everything in her power to take good care of me the best way she knew how, and sharing her family was the primary way. When I was young, she had many health issues, multiple surgeries, and much anxiety due to the divorce, finances, fleeting love affairs, and whatever else she was dealing with at the time. I didn't know all the details, but I saw how hard she tried to take care of me and so I kept things that were troubling me to myself. I couldn't tell her what was happening in school or that I had my own mental anguish. Just looking at Mom let me know that she had enough to deal with on her own. She was always strikingly beautiful, but I could see anxiety in her eyes. I didn't want to go to school, but I went to avoid causing Mom additional stress. As her son, I felt it was my responsibility to take care of her because she was a single parent. But over time, we became codependent. I was excited to go to Egypt during summer vacations and for holidays, because I didn't have to take care of Mom, and I didn't have to worry about her trying to take care of me. It was a vacation from that world for us both.

Traveling between the two worlds my parents lived in made me into a chameleon who took on the characteristics of my environment. I could be Jewish, Christian, or Muslim; aristocratic, average, or athletic. If I blended in, people might not see how different I was. If I was different, they might see all my differences. I stood for nothing but the status quo in any given situation. Little did I know, this was to be the beginning of my political education.

Grandfather Omar was transparent about his world, so I could see it as it was. With him, I often had dinners with prime ministers, heads of state, and dignitaries. Their conversations were preparing me—but for what? I didn't know at the time, but I paid attention. Understanding diversity, different languages, politics, diplomacy, and how to engage with people was just the beginning. I welcomed it because it was my life—in that world. In contrast, my Egyptian world taught me that being a perfect host or dinner guest meant being charming, gracious, and able to navigate or blend into any situation effortlessly. I was educated to avoid uncomfortable conversations by focusing on socially acceptable topics.

Dinner with Grandfather, whether in Cairo, Deauville, Madrid, London, Beverly Hills, or any other work location, exposed me to a majestic world inhabited by film directors, celebrities, royalty, and nobility who would come to his hotel just to dine with him. At first, I didn't know how accomplished his friends were, because I was just a kid. It was from their stories that I began to understand the magnitude of those relationships and the scope of Grandfather's influence and network around the world. If we didn't go to a restaurant, Pepita, who often traveled with us, would prepare a grand, full-course dinner that took hours to finish. The stories and conversations shared around the table weren't in magazines or newspapers; they were private and captivating. At times, Grandfather would show me extravagant gifts, given to him by royal figures, but he liked the modest rather than ostentatious, and usually gave those items away. On occasion, he would hand me a heavy gold watch or an ornate piece of diamond-encrusted jewelry and say, "Give this to your mother." I didn't really know why, but I didn't ask him, either. I understood that his and my grandmother's world was not *the* world. It was one of privilege and sometimes excess. It felt as if there was a competition among their friends to see who had the most beautiful villa with the biggest swimming pool and who played the best golf course or drove the nicest car. People were always waiting to see who could throw the most elaborate event or party to outdo the last. My grandparents didn't subscribe to this world, but they inhabited it.

Faten Hamama was like the Elizabeth Taylor of the Arab world but somewhat less outspoken. She didn't need to speak from podiums, because she could move mountains with the look in her eye or with a faint twist of her upper lip. She didn't go out of the house much, because she'd be mobbed. She was almost a prisoner of her fame. Mostly, our driver, Mohammed, took me out to the Gezira Sporting Club, the Cairo Zoo, the pyramids, or simply to rent videos. On a rare excursion, Grandmother Faten took me to a wedding in Egypt, and we watched the mother of the bride walk serenely down the aisle wearing the largest dress imaginable. When the mother reached the front, the bride jumped out from underneath. I didn't know why but assumed that it symbolized rebirth or becoming a woman. It was so absurd that I wanted to burst out laughing, but Faten elbowed me just as I began chuckling and said, "No, no. Be proper," and then patted my knee in her unique way of scolding me.

The affluent in Egypt did everything that way, and on holidays I lived in that world. The parties were always extravagant with tray-passed hors d'oeuvres, champagne, and other alcohol. They paid attention to the smallest details, making the parties ones to talk about. In Egypt, all ages and generations go to nightclubs or an event at someone's home together. It's not uncommon to see grandparents partying with their children and grandchildren. But because of Egypt's hierarchical society, the friends of my parents and grand-parents wanted their daughters and granddaughters to date Omar and Faten's grandson. I was seen as eligible—even though I knew I wasn't.

———

In elementary school, the bullying began and followed me like a fiery trail of hate. It's odd that the kids in school suspected something I didn't even know for sure yet. The way some of the teachers looked at me made me feel that I was different, that I wasn't normal, and, ultimately, the kids confirmed that I wasn't. I suppose I always thought that I was someone other than whom I appeared to be, but the incessant comments, which turned into persistent bullying, made me acknowledge it to myself. I finally conceded that I wasn't like the other boys, and once I did, society quickly shoved me into a cardboard box, slapped a large label on it, and left me to figure out what to do with myself. Over time, the horrible names I was called—faggot, queer, and homo, among others—ceased to bother me because I could only entertain so much pain.

There were occasions when a few of the teachers looked like they felt bad, but not enough to get involved, until the day one of the kids who regularly called me names pushed me to the ground. Before the fifth grade, no one had physically laid a hand on me or shoved me into a locker, but that afternoon, I knew that if I didn't strike back, the other kids might follow suit and try to beat me up, too. So I stood, balled up my fist, and punched him. It quickly turned into an all-out brawl. Teachers rushed into the schoolyard to break up the fight, pulling us apart. As if that weren't enough, I faced my biggest fear: my parents would be called, told what had happened, and then given the reason I was fighting. I felt sick when the announcement came from the principal, Rabbi Hammerman, calling me into his office along with the other boy. The boy and I sat next to each other in front of Rabbi Hammerman's desk. I didn't know how he was feeling, but my heart thumped against my chest and I clutched the arms of the chair to keep from hurling all over the floor. Being in the principal's office felt horrible because I never wanted to bother anyone. I had taken the verbal abuse day after day, year after year, but I wasn't going to let anyone lay a hand on me. When Rabbi Hammerman came in and shut the door, I prepared for the worst while holding back tears. He sat down, studying both of us and deliberating in silence. He released a heavy sigh and then slowly leaned forward, peering sternly at the other boy.

"Omar is one of the finest and best students I've ever known," he stated firmly. "And if I hear of you calling him a name again, that will be the last of you in this school."

I couldn't believe what I'd heard, and the boy didn't utter a single word in defense. When we were dismissed, I turned to Rabbi Hammerman and said, "Thank you." Even though I was equally at fault, I didn't get into trouble, and he didn't call our parents. He knew I'd been bullied for all of those years in that school, but this time, I think he was proud of me for finally standing up for myself—even if it meant I had to fight.

My childhood was complicated, but it was all I'd ever known, and I lived in and loved both worlds equally. Distant and dissimilar, the only time they ever touched was between my twelfth and thirteenth birthdays.

Between twelve and fifteen is when Muslim boys reach adulthood, or become *baaligh*, and have full responsibility under Islamic law. On the Jewish side, we have a bar mitzvah on our thirteenth birthday to indicate that we have all the rights and obligations of a Jewish adult, including the observation of religious precepts. To celebrate both the Muslim and Jewish traditions of becoming a man, my parents came together and threw me a big party because I belonged to both worlds and taught myself to respect them equally.

Initially, a party wasn't something that I wanted, because Mom told me I should invite all of my friends—and I didn't know where to find any. I knew I didn't have enough for a party, so I started asking random classmates just to make my parents think the other students liked me. I'm sure their parents made them come because of my last name. Grandfather Omar, Dad, his new wife, Shahira—who was pregnant with my baby sister—along with family and friends flew in from Egypt and celebrated with my entire Canadian family. It was so amazing to be surrounded by that much love at one time. There were over two hundred and fifty people laughing, dancing, and telling stories as they enjoyed good food and wine together. On that day, my two worlds were one.

By thirteen my identity was set, and because I was attracted to boys, I wasn't like any of the other boys I knew. Of course, I wasn't attracted to anyone in high school, because I was too busy envying them. I wanted to *be* them. I wanted to be popular and cool, too. I didn't want to be gay and unpopular, or to have my parents find out. I already believed that there was something wrong with me—that I wasn't normal. When Mom spoke with her friends, she called gay people abnormal. When we were walking down the street and she saw someone transgender or someone who dressed alternatively, she'd snicker and call them freaks. The hurt I felt made me want to cower in the shadows and stay there. I didn't know anyone in school who was out, but if anyone was gay, they stayed in the shadows after seeing the way I was bullied.

The only thing I could do was stay muted and withdrawn from people. I was ashamed, and keeping my secret was slowly beginning to kill me. Swallowing the same treatment five consecutive days a week became increasingly challenging. There were days I walked to school instead of taking the bus or carpooling. I needed that time to figure out how I'd make it through the day and who I'd have to avoid, and to convince myself I could deal with the hateful comments, malicious looks, and toxic environment for one more day.

The school bell at the end of the day brought an escape from the students but not from my reality. I'd hurry through the doors, only to be greeted by my mind cruelly recapping the day's events. The residue—and knowing that I had to return for more the next day— left me anxious. A two-day weekend wasn't long enough to recover. I walked through the school halls looking over my shoulder, worried people were talking about me. I hated gym class, even though I was just as good as the other kids. If I missed one catch, kick, or basket, the name-calling started. "Look at him. The little fag can't even catch a ball." If I didn't defend myself, it looked like they were right. If I spoke up, it could turn into something bigger. So I pretended not to hear them, even though I did—every time.

The more popular kids usually left me alone, while the lesser-known kids tried to make a name for themselves, seeking power over me with repetitive teasing and name-calling. I tried to justify it— telling myself that they might be neglected at home and took it out on me. Maybe they were bullied by their own parents or one parent bullied the other, and they mirrored what they saw. Whatever the reasons, it was difficult for me to walk through the corridors without random teenagers asking, "Why aren't you more of a man?" or "Why are you such a woman?" I continued to walk away from confrontation, appearing to be what they said, because I always tried to consider the bigger picture. I had cousins in the same high school, and I worried that they would hear what their friends or other kids were saying about me and tell my aunt, and then Mom would find out.

One cousin had heard the rumors and asked me if I was dating anyone. Just to stop the inquiry from going any further, I replied,

"Yes, I went out with Rachel the other night." The next day, Rachel saw me heading into class and dashed in front of me, blocking the doorway.

"Why would you tell people we were dating?"

When I didn't answer her, she half-smiled, as if she already knew the truth, and walked away. *Why* is the scariest question for a gay boy in the closet because most of the time the honest answer is, *I'm gay.*

The few times I lied to evade such questions or situations, the lies came back to haunt me, so I always felt guilty about defending myself that way. But still, I lied to everyone I loved. It's amazing how one lie turns into two lies, and then into three, becoming a habit or even a lifestyle.

I thought it was best if I stopped saying anything and let people continue to believe whatever they wanted. I ate my feelings, curled up into a fetal position, and tried to sleep as much as I could, immersing myself in cable news or, when alone, *Will & Grace* to avoid thinking about going back to school. I stepped back, deeper into the closet, surrendered to the internal pain, and shut myself out of the life I didn't fit into. Being gay was just too much to bear. My world turned pitch black.

The first time I walked home from school with suicidal thoughts, I'd already written my eulogy in my head. I approached our yellowish-brown apartment building, which was situated diagonally to the Cavendish Mall, the place most of the cool kids hung out. That day, I slowed down until I stood on the sidewalk and stared up toward my ninth-floor apartment. I imagined myself perched on the balcony banister, then releasing my grip and fearlessly plunging to my death. That was one way out of this world. The saddest part of all is that I wasn't scared; I was ready. I drew in the deepest breath I could manage, steadily exhaled, and collected myself. Like every other day, I walked into the building, took the elevator up to our apartment, and went through the daily motions, pretending to be happy and normal while combing through mental pictures of my suicide. Sometimes when I traveled, I hopefully envisioned my plane crashing and imagined Mom running to the crash site, screaming and crying. My suicidal visions were detailed and occupied my thoughts more than they should have. The only reason I didn't kill myself was that I didn't want the people who loved me—as beautifully as both sides of my family did—to suffer. I was afraid of disappointing my parents. As an only child, if I were to die, the Sharif name would not live on.

Most of my formative relationships were from Mom's side of the family. My aunts, uncles, and cousins all had siblings, and I recognized their close bond. I was jealous of those who had siblings because I had none. For years I dreamed of having a sibling of my own—a best friend. When I was fourteen, I was blessed with a baby sister.

I was in Egypt for summer vacation when Fatima was born. It was my stepmother Shahira's first child. I recall the day I went to the hospital to see Fatima for the first time. Dad, Omar, Faten, and other family members and friends were there to welcome her. My sister was incredibly cute. She had pudgy thighs and the most adorable dimples—and I was unbelievably happy. The day Dad and Shahira left the hospital, I went home with them, buzzing with excitement to have a little sister. I knew Shahira would be a great mother because of the way she loved me—as if I were her own son.

The entire time I was with them, I used an old camera to photograph Fatima so I could take her everywhere I went. I'd snap one picture after another, even though she couldn't do anything but lie there and look adorable in whatever little outfit they'd dressed her in.

After summer vacation, I went back to Montreal for school and Dad regularly sent me photos of her smiling and laughing. I couldn't wait until she was old enough to be right by my side. From then on, I had something more to look forward to during the summer and holidays.

I was sitting at my desk one morning in Montreal when a teacher pulled me out of class. My father had called to tell me that he was boarding a private plane from Cairo to Paris. At just four and a half months old, my sister had contracted an unknown virus and became critically ill. The doctors had done everything they could in Egypt, but she wasn't responding to treatment, so they had no recourse but to find another way: a children's hospital in Paris.

When they landed, they rushed Fatima to Necker for surgery. The virus had attacked her organs. Fatima needed a liver transplant, so Dad was donating a piece of his liver—Fatima's only hope to survive. They shaved his stomach, prepped him for surgery, and were about to begin when the doctor canceled the operation; it was too late for Fatima. Dad got out of his hospital bed and went into the room with his wife and infant daughter to find Fatima in an incubator. When he told me the story, his stoic demeanor broke, and he sobbed, unexpectedly, "There were a thousand tubes coming out of her." Fatima passed moments later.

I flew to Paris that same evening to be with family. When I arrived, Catherine picked me up as usual. After dropping off my bags at Le Royal Monceau, where Grandfather Omar was living, we went directly to Dad's flat. The moment I arrived, Dad lifted his shirt to show me where they had shaved his stomach in preparation for surgery. I thought it was odd at the time, but I suppose he wanted me to see that he'd done everything he could to save his daughter. When I went into the bedroom to see Shahira, I found her curled up in bed with the curtains drawn together, balled-up tissue everywhere. The room smelled of sadness and despair. Shahira's pain was indescribable. I closed the doors and let her rest because the right words to comfort her about the loss of her child didn't exist. I would never want my parents to feel that way about me. I owe my life today to the fact that my sister, my guardian angel, died then.

In the eleventh grade, our all-Jewish high school offered the opportunity to take a trip to Poland and Israel. When I learned that the trip would take us to the concentration camps and death camps, I felt compelled to go. To be considered for the trip, students were required to write an essay and complete an interview. I was grateful when my application was accepted, but I wasn't convinced the trip would be a good one. The curiosity to connect to our family history had been inside me for as long as I could remember. The suffering in Bubbie and Zadie's eyes never left them, and this was my opportunity to have a stronger connection to their world and be closer to my history, as horrifying and unsettling as it might be.

When we arrived in Poland, I was conscious of every detail of what we saw. In some of the camps and in the former ghettos, I saw the places Bubbie had vividly described. Majdanek, where Bubbie was separated from her sister and niece, still existed as a preserved landmark and could be restored and made fully operational in a matter of days. I even saw the bunks that my grandmother slept in. Just a glimpse of her world was unnerving. We walked through the death camp and entered rooms with the discarded shoes, hair that had been shaved off, and canisters of Zyklon B gas, used to murder victims. In the back of the camp, under a dome, they kept the ashes of the Jews they had burned in crematoriums. It was bigger than an Olympic-sized pool—like a giant ashtray filled with bodies and bones. As I stared into it, I was covered in perspiration, and my stomach clenched. The bandages were ripped off my memories of the Nazis; with raised eyelids, I shook with horror. Bubbie's sister and her niece were in there.

Bubbie told me that when they were on the train out of the Warsaw Ghetto and heading to the camp, her young niece had nothing to drink and was lying, listless, against her mother—dehydrated and half-dead. They had nothing to offer her, so they spat in a bottle to give her something to drink. When my eyes locked on a bottle sticking out of the ashes in the dome, it made everything all too real. I had a breakdown. I couldn't walk, move, or speak. The teachers didn't think I'd make it through the rest of the trip and contemplated sending me home. I had lost my faith in humanity; Bubbie's eternal light of optimism had extinguished within me. How could people be so cruel? As we took the bus to the next city, Gill, a popular girl in my grade, who I always assumed made fun of me like everyone else, came and sat next to me. She placed my head on her lap and held me for the next four hours as I cried. An unlikely friendship was born that reignited my faith in the goodness of others.

———

After spending time in Poland, visiting sites where death and devastation took place, we flew to Israel for a week to celebrate vibrant, modern Jewish life. I was moved by the energy and spirituality in the air, and I felt my own healing taking place. Regardless of what religion I subscribed to, the land felt sacred, like it belonged to the world—to everyone. We went to the Old City of Jerusalem, where I saw the four sections, the Christian Quarter, Jewish Quarter, Muslim Quarter, and Armenian Quarter, each of which celebrated their differences and uniqueness while united by circumstance and geography. It was a beautiful mosaic of how the world could be and of how I saw myself. That trip left me hopeful that I would see rebirth after devastation. Despite challenges and political upheaval, spring always follows winter, the light comes after the darkness, and hate can turn to hope. It was clear to me that people can overcome anything. Maybe this, too, is what Omar always meant when he said, "Put your losses behind you; tomorrow we win!" Omar and Bubbie were optimists, and I was learning how to be one, too.

On the ten-hour flight home from Israel, I was sitting in an emergency exit row of the 747 aircraft. Midflight, a handsome El Al flight attendant in his mid-twenties named Tomer caught my attention. He was sitting in the jump seat directly facing me, and he made sure I noticed him by appearing to accidentally brush his foot against mine. At one point, I got up and went to the back of the plane to ask for some water. Most of the students were asleep. Without warning, the flight attendant grabbed me around my waist, pulled me into a lavatory, and kissed me. I had never kissed or touched another man in that way. He undid his pants and placed my hand inside them. I was too panicked to be excited; literally everyone I knew from high school was on the plane. Not worth the risk! I said in Hebrew, "I can't. I want to, but I can't." I made him pull up his pants and open the door. When he did, I stood face-to-face with the most popular and gossipy girl in school. I stepped out of the bathroom, followed by the flight attendant, and a giant grin ripped across her freckled face. Rumors were swirling by the time the plane landed. I didn't think anyone actually believed her and, fortunately, I didn't have to go to school and deal with it, because I found out I had mono soon after. I didn't know if it was stress or if I caught the so-called kissing disease from the first guy I ever kissed. I stayed home from school for a month and went back the final week before graduating—but by then, the rumors had multiplied.

On the last day of school, I was walking down the hall, and a group of guys walked past me. One of them snickered, "Homo." Another asked, "Why are you so feminine?" For the first time, I responded, knowing I was about to graduate and wouldn't have to see them again. I said, "Maybe because I was raised by a single mother." I turned around and walked away. An hour later two of those boys came up and said, "We're really sorry. We shouldn't have said that." I stood in the corridor wondering if I should have defended myself earlier. Maybe all this time, they hadn't known that their words actually hurt me.

That night, I sat out on the balcony waiting for Mom to come home. I looked out into the darkness, wondering how many others were hiding secrets so that they could feel accepted by those around them. Bubbie's mother had once reassured her, "My child, if you live, there will one day exist a free world for us." I had to live to see this free world my great-grandmother spoke of. One day, perhaps I could be free of fear, of ridicule, free to live in the open, and free from thoughts of suicide and death. If Bubbie and Zadie had survived so much worse, I could survive this.

3

Funny Boy

Being home in Egypt gave me much-needed time with Dad, Shahira, and Grandmother during summer vacations. But the year after graduating from high school was particularly special. Dad and Shahira had another baby to pour their love into, and I had a brother, Karem. I was happy for them, and it was nice to see Shahira smile again. I was grateful to have another sibling, and although we were sixteen years apart, Karem was my future partner in crime.

Dad and his family were proper and rarely showed affection; they loved me differently from the way my mother's family did. They didn't ask personal questions or appear to worry about me being shy and reticent. I was a little more outgoing in Egypt than I was in Canada because they didn't constantly smother or judge me. No one really knew much about me, as the focus was always on my grandparents. I didn't have to fight or evade anyone, but I still had to be careful.

I spent my first seven weeks in Egypt that summer interacting

with family and their close group of friends. We usually played back-
gammon and cards by the side of the pool or under the cabana on the
beach. Grandmother Faten was private, and unless she was working,
her preference was to be at one of her beach homes in El Gouna on
the Red Sea or in Sahel on the Mediterranean coast. Besides her talent for acting, she had a knack for investing in real estate. Her homes
were always serene and exquisite—just like her. Being with Faten was
a vacation in and of itself, filled with luxuries, fishing trips, good
food, and love.

In the evening, I'd take our Jeep Sahara and drive over to meet
up with my friend, Karim, who was just a few years older than me. I
didn't have a driver's license, but it didn't seem to matter. I somehow
always felt I was above the law in Egypt; until I came out, just using
my grandparents' names was a get-out-of-jail-free card. When I'd pull
up to Karim's house, he'd jump in the front seat, and we'd head over
to the one nightclub in town. The Arena was a circular coliseum with
layered seating and a large, open-air dance floor in the middle that
sometimes doubled as an outdoor movie theater, making it a favorite
gathering spot and the heart of resort nightlife. Occasionally, Karim's
sister joined us, along with her boyfriend. We'd have fun dancing and
drinking to excess before calling it a night.

One evening, the four of us ended up hanging out with a group
of girls who were visiting from Ireland. By the end of the evening,
one of them had shown interest in both Karim and me. Caitlin was a
pretty girl, with light freckles, emerald eyes, and blond hair trimmed
evenly above her shoulders. It was evident that a lot of guys were
interested in her, and she appeared to appreciate their attention, but
Caitlin made it clear that she was going home with one of us.

In Egypt, friendships often exist within the social circles of one's parents, so when Caitlin started telling people she liked me, I knew I'd have to respond. Over the years, no one had ever seen me date a girl or known of me being intimate with one. The fact that I was a virgin wasn't reason enough to prevent me from having an interest in Caitlin. If I didn't show interest, I could be one rumor away from someone knowing my secret or for bullying to become my reality in Egypt, too. Conceding to peer pressure and to the fear of losing my final refuge, I left the nightclub with Caitlin at around three thirty that morning and drove toward her hotel. We'd barely driven a few blocks when Caitlin jumped into the backseat, kicked her shoes off, and slipped out of her jeans.

"Come on," she said, pulling her light blue top over her head.

I parked the Jeep and climbed in the back seat, trembling. I didn't want to rush anything, because I was still a virgin, but I didn't feel comfortable telling Caitlin that. Trying to create small talk, I asked her if she'd had fun at the nightclub. She leaned in and kissed me. From there, I just let her lead. I thought to myself, *maybe I can do this*—maybe I can hide forever, maybe it's just a phase. But when I entered her, all I remember thinking is how she opened up just like a Birkin bag—quite possibly the gayest thought one could have during heterosexual intercourse.

Afterward, I dropped Caitlin off at her hotel and hoped I wouldn't have to see her again. I did all that just to keep my secret, but it wasn't worth it. That wasn't the way I'd wanted to have sex for the first time.

The last I heard of Caitlin, she had returned to Ireland. At least there wouldn't be any questions about whether I had an interest in girls. After that experience, I took a step back and avoided conversations with my friends about sex for the rest of my teen years. I decided that the next time I had sex, I would choose the person and the place.

———

I was with Grandfather Omar for the remainder of my vacation, and it was during my teenage years that we began to travel together more frequently. My physical changes were more noticeable, and so were the reactions that men had toward me, especially in the Middle East and North Africa. In more conservative and repressive countries like Egypt, Tunisia, Morocco, and others, men are not supposed to have sex with women until they get married, and they can't marry until they have enough saved for a dowry, which isn't easy to accomplish with modest wages. In these societies, countless gay and straight men alike view companionship and sex with men as simply a form of release—and if they "top," they're not gay. Sometimes these men looked for tourists in the streets to lure into the shadows, where they made their move. I was a local, but because I was light skinned, with light eyes, I looked more like a tourist.

One afternoon, Grandfather Omar and I were in Luxor, shopping on the bank of the Nile, when I noticed a little tourist shop. The stone and terra-cotta-colored buildings on the street stood out just enough to distinguish themselves from the desert sands. No sooner had I darted inside to look at its wares than a shopkeeper followed me into the store, and without uttering a word, he grabbed at me, quickly exposing himself. This behavior was typical for men. They did this regularly to me in souks or even in taxis with prayer beads hanging from the rearview mirror.

Often, security guards or military police would catcall, trying to get me to follow them into a parking garage or somewhere out of plain sight. For the most part, I was shocked and confused. As I grew older, I sometimes got a little excited when showed that kind of attention, but I didn't really understand what I was feeling or what I was supposed to feel. I never yelled at them in Arabic, because I knew they thought I was a tourist or a visitor, and I was worried I'd get in trouble if these officers knew I was Egyptian—and it crossed my mind that I might be doing something wrong, too. Most of the time I ran away, and a couple of times I acquiesced, but I couldn't tell anyone, or they might suspect that those men saw something in me to solicit that reaction. Then, they'd know my secret.

———

Before starting college that fall, my cousin Mikey and his friends had planned a ten-day backpacking trip through Greece to launch their next life chapter. As we'd always been close, Mikey invited me along. Mikey knew I was always up for an adventure, and I wanted to spend time with him before he went off to school. My father agreed to let me go and covered the cost of my trip. One of his friends, Naldo, gave me a thousand euros for spending money, and Grandmother Faten and Aunt Nadia added heavily to the fund, telling me to have a great time.

I flew from Cairo to Athens a day ahead of Mikey and his friends, Lindsey and Rob. When they arrived, the fun began. We went sightseeing, enjoyed traditional Greek dishes, and hit the bars and clubs. The next thing on our itinerary was a ferry to Mykonos, one of the Cyclades islands. When the ferry docked, I couldn't wait to explore. We walked the narrow streets, spent time on the beaches, grabbed lunch, and took everything in. It didn't take long before I realized that Mykonos was an alluring paradise for gay men. People were carefree and happy—I'd never seen anything like it. No one had to

hide—they were out in plain sight, holding hands, kissing, and showing affection for one another. It didn't matter where we went—there
weren't any shadows.

I was sure by now that Mikey had heard rumors about me, but my
cousin didn't mention them or even hint at anything. Mikey didn't
judge me. He just let me enjoy being myself and free. After we went
to a couple of straight bars that first evening, I ventured off solo so
I could discover more. For the next few nights, I could feel myself
breathing serenely.

After leaving Mykonos, we took the ferry to Santorini, another of
the Cyclades islands. The rugged landscape was shaped by a volcanic
eruption, and the city was built on a downward slope facing the Ae-
gean Sea. There were charming and picturesque homes, white with
blue rooftops, resting on the cliffs. The colorful sunsets were painted
with the most perfect strokes I'd ever seen. Its breathtaking views
made Santorini the ideal place for lovebirds and honeymooners. But
even with all its beauty, it didn't compare to Mykonos. Mykonos felt
like a community—a home I'd never known.

The next day, the four of us were in line to board a ferry to the
party island of Ios. Our plans were to enjoy a few days there and then
head home. I glanced around, observing my surroundings while we
waited, and a small waterplane caught my attention. The sign in front
of it read MYKONOS. I turned to Mikey with the widest grin imaginable and said, "This isn't my island . . . *that's* my island," pointing
excitedly at the sign. I gave Mikey a big hug, said bye to his friends,
and without further explanation, I slung my large orange and black
backpack over my shoulder, jumped out of line, and made a dash toward a makeshift booth near the airplane. Sounding as though I was
trying to escape someone, I asked the middle-aged guy behind the

counter, "Do you have room for one more?" Folding the newspaper he was reading, he said, "You're the last." I paid him fifty euros, took my ticket, and boarded the plane. I was going back to paradise.

I didn't have a hotel reservation or a place to stay, but I knew I'd figure it out. I hadn't planned to return, but the island called me back like a siren beckoning a lost sailor. When I arrived, I went from one hotel to another, looking for a room until I found one. I checked in, put my backpack in the comfortable seaside room, and set out on adventure. I stopped at the receptionist's desk and asked him where to begin. He pulled a small flyer out of his pocket, handed it to me, and pointed. "I recommend that you go here. There's a party at Super Paradise this afternoon; I'm sure you'll make some friends." I rented a Vespa and drove toward my destination.

I parked the Vespa, followed the music toward the beach, and removed my sandals as soon as I stepped off the paved path. The vibe was chill and relaxed, the way I wanted the rest of the world to be—whole and one. There were gay and straight people partying together on the beach and sexuality was a non-issue. People didn't stare or point, whisper or gawk. Everyone was equal—LGBTQ and allies alike.

After taking a swim in the bay, I laid my towel on a lounge chair as my toes sank into the pebbles of sand. I stretched out to bask in the warmth of the sun, but before I was settled, a slim, toned guy wearing a dark blue Speedo helped himself to the other chair under my umbrella. Until then, I'd only seen other guys wear board shorts, but when I looked around, I realized I was the only one wearing them on this beach.

"G'day, mate."

"Hi," I replied.

"I'm Adrian. And you are?" he asked, seductively scanning my body.

"Omar."

"Nice to meet you, Omar. So, what brings you to Mykonos?"

I wanted to say, "The same thing that brought you here," but I didn't. I said, "Initially, I came here to hang out with friends."

"Initially? Are they still here with you?" he asked, looking around to see if anyone was approaching.

"Not anymore. My cousin and his friends went to Ios, and I decided I wanted to be here. I like this island," I admitted, as I watched the ocean spill onto the shore with its own rhythm and timing.

"I like it here, too." After a brief pause, he added, "You're quite handsome."

I didn't respond, because that wasn't something I was used to hearing. Adrian was handsome, Australian, in his early twenties, and built like a soccer player. I listened to Adrian tell me about himself and his job as a flight attendant for Emirates. He seemed to be worldly, friendly, and good-natured. When he spoke, it was refreshing to hear him talk openly about whatever he wanted. He didn't have to say he was gay, because there was no reason to hide or explain it. He wasn't shy or uncomfortable with his sexuality, either—at least not on Mykonos. Unlike me, Adrian didn't appear to be hiding a secret at all. At sixteen, I hadn't reached that level of comfort, and I wasn't sure I ever would. But the island didn't have closets, and until I left, I was free to explore being me.

"How old are you?"

"Seventeen," I lied. "But I'm going to university soon," I added, realizing I had just admitted I was a minor but failing miserably to make myself appear more mature.

Adrian suddenly got up and said, "Let's go!"

"Where?"

"You're on school break. It's hot out here, right?" I nodded in agreement. "So, let's get some ice cream and explore."

As the day progressed, I grew more comfortable with Adrian. He bought us some ice cream, and we walked the beach until the heat became unbearable, forcing us to take a swim to cool off. When we emerged from the ocean, we stood there with the waves flushing over our feet. Adrian moved closer to me until I could feel his breath on my lips—as if he was asking for permission. With the warmth of the sun on my back, I leaned in, and he kissed me. I abandoned any thoughts I had and really let myself go for the first time. We went back to my hotel, and long story short, we found out exactly what I was willing to do for a Klondike bar . . . and it was wonderful.

The next morning, I headed down to the lobby to ask the concierge if he knew about anything exciting happening on the island that day. Thoroughly prepared for my question, he recited a variety of activities and parties taking place on the beaches and at some of the local bars. When I turned around to leave, I ran into a group of guys who were staying at the same hotel. After some casual conversation, they asked if I was with someone. When I told them I was alone, they invited me to hang with them and explore the island. After getting to know them, I gravitated toward Rayan, a good-looking Jordanian in his late twenties. He told me a lot about himself, including that he worked as a dentist. The more we learned about one another, the more drawn to each other we became. I think it was mostly because of our shared Arab background, but his brawny and rugged appearance wasn't a deterrent, either. A few hours later, my phone vibrated. I glanced at the message, realizing that I'd forgotten about Adrian.

He invited me to hang out with him, but I didn't know what to say, because I was exactly where I wanted to be at that moment. I really liked Rayan and had wanted to get to know more about him since he'd captured my attention—and when I looked up at him, he still had it. I put my phone away without sending a reply. Following a long day of activities, dinner, and dancing, I was sure I wanted to spend the night with Rayan. And that night turned into another.

I found myself in an emotional triangle with both Adrian and Rayan. My interest was unquestionably in Rayan, but I didn't feel right ignoring Adrian's message. I wanted to be polite to him, as he was the first guy I'd met on the island—and the first guy I'd ever slept with—so I agreed to hang out with him again.

On the fourth night, while Adrian and I were heading into a restaurant for dinner, we ran into Rayan, and his disappointment was palpable.

"Hey."

"I tried to reach you," he told me.

"I was planning to call you tonight."

"I'm sure. It seems you've been enjoying the island today," he said, eyeing Adrian.

"We were just sightseeing. Nothing else, really."

Rayan tucked his hands into his pockets, kind of shrugged, and then he was gone.

In the end, nothing worked out with either Adrian or Rayan. I didn't expect to leave Mykonos with a boyfriend, but I accomplished more than I'd ever thought possible. I had discovered and freely explored a whole new side of myself. Maybe I didn't find love, but I did find within myself permission to love.

After I returned to Egypt, Dad and I went to see Omar in France before I flew home to Canada. In my world, I'd become a little more comfortable with who I was, although no one knew any different.

———

Eleventh grade concluded high school, but Quebec required two years of CEGEP—the equivalent of a general or vocational college—before attending university. I went to Marianopolis College and studied liberal arts. The college was run by Catholic nuns and different from the all-Jewish high school I had previously attended. In the cafeteria, students from different backgrounds and ethnic groups would separate themselves and sit together in sections. The Jews occupied the tables near the front, the Italians behind them, the Greek students behind them, and the Arabs were on the side near the windows. On the first day of CEGEP, I felt torn as to where to sit. I wondered if I should sit with the Jewish kids—some of whom had bullied me in high school—or with the Arabs. I made the decision to alternate sitting between both groups. Less than two weeks after CEGEP began, the eastern United States was hit by the September 11 attacks. The atmosphere in the classroom grew heavy and emotions were momentarily suppressed by shock. Paralyzed with fear, everyone had gathered around a television in the student lounge to watch the developments unfold. As the newscaster explained what happened, a group of Arab students began to cheer.

"We got them," yelled one Lebanese student.

I turned to him and retorted, "You got who? Someone's father, someone's brother, someone's sister, someone's child—who exactly did you get?"

He turned, pushed me, and replied, "The Americans . . . and the

Jews," while looking me up and down accusingly. I shook my head in disgust and walked away.

Classes were canceled for the rest of the day. People were heading home in a somber, sedated state. No one said anything to me. I left campus and drove home to watch the rest of the coverage with my mother.

———·———

That November, Grandfather Zadie was diagnosed with cancer. Our family quickly rallied together the way he'd always taught us and took round-the-clock watches at the hospital for seven months. All of Zadie's children and I took six-hour shifts to fill every hour of each week, so he was never alone. We wanted to make sure he felt the love he'd generously given to each of us. In May, Zadie lost his battle with cancer. Although everyone rallied around Bubbie, she seemed lost and lonely without Zadie. It was equally hard to watch Mom struggle with the loss of her father. I delivered his eulogy at the funeral in Yiddish and was grateful for the opportunity to express what he meant to me—to all of us.

———·———

I was fortunate that my friend Tyler attended the same CEGEP. An accidental meeting brought us together during my first exposure at sixteen to Montreal's LGBTQ community in a nightclub aptly named Unity. The club was so dark I could barely see anyone, like the space was meant to be hidden, and so I felt safe—and I loved the music. They mostly played dance remixes from the 90s. I'd sit at the bar, hoping I looked like I fit in, and watch everyone dancing and getting along like a community—one that I wasn't yet a part of. When a guy came over and offered to buy me a drink, I declined. I was too shy, especially in Montreal. I stayed an hour or so longer as a spectator and then felt that I should leave. I was worried about running into someone I knew, and I wasn't yet ready for the consequences. I was always looking over my shoulder, and hiding made it hard to have fun. I headed down the stairs to leave and bumped into Tyler, who was a year older than me. He grew up next door to my cousins, Mitchell and Lisa, in Westmount. When we locked eyes, my lips tightly pressed together, and I had the sudden urge to run, but neither of us moved. I thought I'd finally screwed up but fought off the dread when I realized there was nothing to fear—we shared the same secret.

Tyler and I became best friends and started going to Unity regularly. I'd tell Mom I was going out with other friends from school to keep her from suspecting anything. I'd drive over to Tyler's house, pick him up, and head for the place we were welcomed as is. When I was out late, friends like Gill were sound alibis.

Until then, I had rarely spoken about myself, because I couldn't tell the truth. With Tyler, I could talk about anything and everything without lying. Unity gave us a place to let go and be ourselves while dancing to the emboldening songs of Celine Dion and Whitney Houston. "Greatest Love of All," by Houston, was about loving yourself. That year, while I was searching for my authentic self, that song became my anthem.

By the winter of 2002, Tyler and I had started going out more. I was still discovering who I was and finally becoming more comfortable, but being out in public still felt risky. It didn't take long before I realized that I was at risk in a different type of way, too. For the first time in my life, I was going out on dates. I met a Jewish guy online who was handsome, affluent, and from the same general community as me. I tried to learn as much about him as I could. After a few weeks chatting, we agreed to meet in person. Donnie invited me to his fashionable loft in the Plateau, a hipster neighborhood in a Francophone part of the city.

From the onset of our conversations, I knew Donnie was a guy's guy, but I wasn't sure what to expect. When Donnie answered the door, he looked like he belonged in a 90s boy band. He was five eleven, with a muscular physique and deep blue eyes, and wearing a red bandana tied around his forehead that pulled the jet-black and flowy hair away from his face. When Donnie invited me inside, we sat down and started talking. After a while, one thing led to another, and that thing led to sex. At the end of the night, I left feeling encouraged that this could lead to something. After my last class the following day, I sent him a text to feel things out.

Donnie replied, "Can you come by tonight?"

I wasn't expecting an invite so soon, but I texted back, "Sure."

I slipped my book into my backpack, zipped it up, and headed over to his place.

When I arrived, the routine was pretty much the same as the previous night, and again, we hooked up. I knew it was getting late, and I had classes the next morning, so I told Donnie I had to go. As I was walking toward the door, Donnie grabbed my shoulder and said, "Hold on. I want to show you something." It was strange because he sounded nervous and he was acting like something was wrong. He went into his bedroom, and I followed closely behind him. He opened his closet door, knelt down, reached to the back, and started digging for something. He pulled out a brown shoebox with a blue lid and stood up, holding it as if he wasn't sure he wanted to reveal its contents.

"Is that what you want to show me?" I asked, pointing at the box, expecting it to be filled with old love letters or something.

He walked over to me and removed the lid.

"You see this?" he stated in a harsh tone, making me uncomfortable.

I leaned in, peeked inside the box, and took a soft step backward after seeing the gun.

"Yeah," I replied, forcing that singular word out of my mouth while my heart rate steadily increased. I could hear the thumping of my pulse. Tiny beads of sweat were forming on my brow, but I didn't wipe them away.

It was strange that Donnie had a gun because in Canada gun laws are more strict and handguns less common than in the States. But at that moment, I didn't care where he got it or why he had it. All I wanted was to get away as quickly as possible.

As I inched backwards, Donnie took steps closer and said, "I pulled this on the last guy who threatened to out me. I know you're not going to tell anyone about us, are you?"

"Of course not. Why would I?"

He nodded, signaling I could go.

Trying to act normal, I turned around and got out of there. I jogged down the stairs and over to my car like everything was fine. I jumped in the driver seat, locked the doors, and turned the ignition. When I pulled off, Donnie was still standing in his doorway with the box in his hands.

I felt like I couldn't drive away fast enough from Donnie or his gun. He didn't want to come out of the closet, so he pulled a gun out of it instead. He hadn't come around to fully accepting who he was, and it was unnerving to realize that his fear had manifested into him actually threatening my life. I felt light-headed and needed to pull over, but I was too afraid to stop. I shook for the entire drive home.

When I completed my second year of the CEGEP in 2003, I received acceptance letters from all the universities I applied to other than Harvard and Yale. My family was happy that McGill was one of them, because they wanted me to stay in Montreal. Dad offered to get me an apartment so I wouldn't have to live at home anymore. Even though I'd have more privacy in my own place, after my trip to Mykonos, I wanted to go to a school outside of Montreal where I could feel totally free. I loved Montreal, but I still didn't want my family to know my secret, and if I stayed it would eventually come out. I wasn't escaping my family or all the beautiful aspects the city had to offer—I was fleeing my own internal anxiety and the fear that came with it.

———

For as long as I can remember, reading the morning paper and watching the news has been part of my daily routine. I took an interest in politics early, naturally curious about global events and the way the world was governed. My decision to pursue political studies at Queen's University in Kingston kept me true to my passion.

Kingston was a college town about three hours away from Montreal. I didn't know anyone there, and no one knew me, either. Queen's was a conservative university that provided the opportunity for me to start fresh, and I did just that, even though I didn't consider myself a particularly conservative person.

Attempting to relinquish the labels from my past, I created a persona of who I wanted to be so that I wouldn't be victimized all over again. I decided that when I got to Queen's University, I was going to be popular and known the way I wanted to be—losses in the past; today I win. I didn't know what caused kids to single me out in elementary and high school, but I decided I wasn't going to look weak. I rationalized that if I looked tougher physically, my peers would think I was tougher emotionally. I took eyeliner and drew a scar on the left side of my face, covering it with small pieces of medical tape. I folded a bandana and tied it around my head, like Donnie—it was definitely a look. I told everyone I met that my name was Junior, and like a reality TV star, Junior was funny, irreverent, and the life of the party, with an unlimited budget.

The first week of school, Frosh Week, was a welcome to the university. They had a variety of activities to facilitate student gatherings, and that's how I met Cayla. We were hanging out in my dorm room, talking about the activities and getting to know one another. At the end of the night, we casually ended up sleeping together, but we didn't have sex. I was excited to hear from Cayla when she called a few days later. I thought she wanted to hang out again, but she actually informed me that she had crab lice and that I should go get checked. I was always so afraid of what I could contract from a man that it never dawned on me I could get something from a woman. I hung up the phone and immediately went to the Queen's health center. I was taken into a little room and instructed to get undressed. A few minutes later I stood there, naked and numb, while the doctor examined my genitals and pubic hair with popsicle sticks.

At one point the doctor looked up and said, "Well, I don't see anything. Come back in a week and we'll check again because the lice could still be in the larva or egg stage. I don't want you to buy a prescription and spend money on shampoo if you don't need to—"

"I beg your pardon," I interrupted. "Now's not the time to be frugal with my money, okay? I am not mother hen, and I'm not going to sit on my eggs until they hatch. Just write the damn prescription."

I went to the pharmacy to buy the shampoo, along with a little comb. While I was looking over the counter, I noticed mattress spray. The pharmacist told me that I only needed one bottle for an entire apartment, but I bought four bottles for my small dorm room with a shared bathroom. That night, I waited for everyone on the floor to go to sleep, and then sprayed the contents of the bottles everywhere. Mattress, carpets, sheets, clothes, walls, light fixtures, the computer—everything. I was both mortified and disgusted at the same time. While spraying, I thought to myself, "I'm going to kill every living thing in this building," and I nearly did.

Within ten minutes, the fumes were so heavy from the spray that they set off the smoke detector and all the alarms in Albert Hall. Everyone had to evacuate the building in the middle of the night and wait for the firemen and paramedics. It didn't take long for rumors to float around that the firemen could pinpoint the room where the smoke detector had gone off. As humiliating as the situation was, I went over to one of the resident hall managers, who was talking with a fireman and admitted, "I think it was my room, but there wasn't a fire, and I wasn't smoking or doing drugs." The next day, it seemed that everyone had heard that I single-handedly emptied out the dorms. When I walked into the cafeteria, people whispered and laughed, but it was funny enough and fit with the persona I had created, so I just embraced it. I even bought a T-shirt that said, I GOT CRABS AT HERBS. From that point on, I was famous on campus. People would point and say, "Hey! There's Crab Lice Boy."

I was starting to make friends on campus, and no one suspected I was gay—because, hey, I got crabs from a girl in my first week at college. Three weeks in, I became a little more exploratory, and I met a fourth-year student named Chris on gay.com. He invited me to hang out at his off-campus housing that Saturday, telling me that his housemates would be out at the bars. The area he lived in was known as the student ghetto. After freshman year, groups of students often rent a house together near campus. Since it wasn't far, I walked over to his place. When Chris answered the door, he looked exactly like his photos. He was incredibly muscular, with short, spiky brown hair and indigo eyes. He looked like a sexy, fit farmer from the prairie provinces of Canada. I hadn't been at Queen's long, and until that point, I hadn't met anyone that was gay. There weren't any gay bars in Kingston, at least none that I'd heard about. What Kingston did have was seven prisons, a military base, and three post-secondary institutions, including a military college.

The building he lived in looked like a fraternity house that concealed a wealth of student history; I was sure that new groups of students left their own contributions one year after another. When I took a few steps inside, the floorboards creaked loudly, making my presence known. The large living room was off to the right, and the kitchen was directly behind it. Empty beer bottles cluttered countertops, bookshelves, and what seemed like every open space. There was a flight of stairs that led to the second floor, but Chris motioned to a door beside them that led me downstairs to the basement, where he slept. We sat on his unmade bed playing video games, drinking beer, and talking a little. The rest of the time we spent making out. I opted not to have sex with him because his penis was larger than any I had seen before; I was worried I might get turned inside-out, like a sock fresh out of the laundry. Chris promised to use lubricant, but I told him not to come near me unless he was offering an epidural. Around midnight, the door slammed shut above our heads and the floorboards creaked as though a herd of cattle was being led into the house.

"I thought you said your housemates were at the bars," I reminded him.

"Yeah. The guys aren't supposed to be home this early. I don't know what's going on," he said.

What I didn't know was that Chris played on the football team and lived in what was known as the football house. Chris was unusually calm, despite the fact that he wasn't out to his teammates. His confident reply let me know it wasn't a big deal—to him.

"Don't worry about it," he told me. "You can spend the night and leave before everyone wakes up."

No sooner had he made the offer then the guys started pounding on his door, yelling in sync for Chris to come out and chill with them.

Chris yelled back, "No! I'm tired. I've got to get some rest," but the guys were persistent and continued banging on the door.

I panicked and insisted, "I have to leave. I'm sorry. I just have to go."

He said, "How are you going to accomplish that without going out the same way you came in? And I'm not okay with that at this point. Are you? Just wait until everyone goes to bed."

I hadn't met that many people online, and I certainly hadn't spent the night with anyone from the internet after my first time meeting them. While he was trying to get me to sit down and relax, I was looking for another way out of the basement, and the window in the top corner of his room was it.

"Lift me up and help me through that window," I suggested.

He smiled and replied in a sensible tone, "Junior, you're never getting through that window."

But I was filled with useless information from my cousin Mitchell, and I insisted that I'd heard if your head can fit through a space, your entire body can fit through it, too.

"Just hoist me up," I demanded.

He propped open the window, lifted me off the floor, and pushed. When my hands hit the ground, I attempted to pull myself through the small frame. It took about sixty seconds to realize that the information I had heard was probably about mice and not about men. I had part of the information correct, because my head went through, but I got stuck at my hips.

"Just come back in," Chris laughed.

"No! Push harder," I instructed. He tried, unsuccessfully, so I insisted more sternly, "Tuck the fat in. Just tuck it in! We can get there if you just—tuck—it—in!"

After all his pushing and my wiggling, I was lodged so tightly in place that I wasn't going in or out of that window. I could only imagine what the view was from the inside—just an ass and two dangling legs coming through the top of a wall. The numbness and tingling in my legs and toes cautioned that I was losing circulation.

"You have to go get help," I said, sounding pitiful. I wasn't going anywhere, it had started to rain, and I was lying in dirt that was quickly turning into thick, black mud.

"I'll be right back."

"Wait, wait, wait. Where are you going?"

"I'll get Matt. He'll help. He's a good guy."

"Can we trust him?"

"We have to if you want to get out of there."

Chris jogged upstairs and quickly returned with his housemate, Matt. I was mortified by the incident and the optics. When I told Matt that the sensation in my legs was nearly gone, he grabbed and lifted them.

"Why didn't you go out the front door?" Matt asked.

"Because the window was closer. Now, would you please just help get me out of here?" I begged.

Within seconds, I heard more chatter coming from the room and knew the rest of the housemates were behind me, taking in the view. Eventually, one of them called the fire department.

When the firemen came, they worked quickly to unscrew the frame from the window and break it off my body. When one of the firemen finally pulled me to a standing position, my legs were barely functioning, and the street was full of onlookers. I stood eye to eye with the same fireman from the crab lice incident just a couple weeks prior. He shook his head and chuckled in disbelief.

"Junior, right?" he said, recalling my name. "I see you're going to be keeping us busy for the next four years."

From that point on, there was no hiding. Three weeks in and that story spread across campus. The decision had been made for me; I was out—if not from the closet, then from the window. Not only was I gay—I was a hot mess. I regularly found myself in the most absurd situations, and somehow it only endeared me to others—because it was honest. Even the guys on the football team couldn't help but laugh about it, only this time it wasn't in a condescending way. This time, people were laughing with me—not at me.

That night, I learned about acceptance—those football jocks became my closest friends and remain so to this day. Brad was a Canadian all-star wide receiver, the son of a conservative senator, and had no reason to become my best friend, but he did, and without judgment. From that day on, I became an honorary member of the team. Where they went, I went, whether it was to practices and games, out for pizza, or to the bars. I'd walk up to the bar, lay out my dad's credit card, and order a hundred and fifty vodka sodas, six nights a week. We weren't at every party—we *were* every party. I quickly befriended the hockey, rugby, and lacrosse players, too. Because everyone followed the football players' lead, just by association, students treated me with respect. There was a hierarchy of popularity, and because I was at the top, it was uncool to call me gay or make jokes about me. Because of friends like Brad, Cliff, Graham, Dixon, Thaine, and Mo and others, I finally felt like I fit in—without secrets.

I'd always been a Montreal Canadiens fan, and that year, Montreal faced Boston in the first round of the NHL playoffs. Just before the second game of the series was about to start, I saw a guy wearing a Bruins hat in the cafeteria while I proudly donned my Canadiens jersey. As the Bruin approached me in the crowd, I stuck out my chest, locked my shoulders and walked into him, like a body check, knocking over whatever was on his tray. The Canadiens made a miraculous recovery that series, falling three games to one, only to come back to win it all in seven. I'd found the Boston boy's number in the school directory, and after each game of the comeback, I left him an overbearing message, mimicking the voice of Matt Damon in *Good Will Hunting*: "How do you like them apples?" The Bruin's name was Raphael, or Raph, and he grew up outside of Boston. For some reason or other, Raph *did* like them apples. We became best friends, and Raph eventually began rooting for the Canadiens, too. In return, I went to all his lacrosse games to cheer him on.

Many of the guys on the Queen's athletic teams told me that they had never met an openly gay person, but they quickly became my protectors and never let anyone say a negative word about me. If someone tried, they were quick to defend me. We'd travel annually on spring break to Mexico and the Caribbean together. For as much as I taught them about diversity and inclusion, they taught me more about self-respect and how to embrace my authentic self.

A few months later, Grandfather Omar invited me to the film premiere of his latest movie, *Hidalgo*. It was my first time going to Los Angeles, and the Academy Awards were taking place that same weekend. The night I arrived, we went to a pre-party at the Hollywood Hills mansion of New Line Cinema's co-chairman Bob Shaye, where Grandfather introduced me to several of his old friends and peers, including Sean Connery. During casual conversations and spontaneous introductions, I met Cathy. She was exceedingly kind and showed interest in the details of my visit—apparently aware that I was Omar Sharif's grandson. After Steven Tyler solicited my assistance to help him find his daughter, Liv, Cathy escorted me around the party and introduced me to everyone else, A-list celebrities and actors I'd seen on television or in the movies, if I hadn't already met them at one of Grandfather's dinners.

Since Grandfather had given me tickets to all the major parties, including the *Vanity Fair* party at Morton's The Steakhouse the next night, I invited Cathy and her friend Jess Cagle, whom I was secretly crushing over, to come with me. Everyone who was anyone was there, including Paris Hilton, Charlize Theron, Donald and Melania Trump, and more. Again, Cathy escorted me around the party, introducing me to everyone, and everyone knew her. What I didn't realize was that she wrote for the Liz Smith column of the *New York Post*. Cathy neatly orchestrated the chance for me to take Paris Hilton to Grandfather's premiere the next night as my date, but she was ultimately unable to attend. When I returned to Queen's University, there were articles written that I had dated Paris Hilton, and although it wasn't true, it cemented my reputation at the university for the three years to come. I had become the person I wanted to be while driving to Queen's on that first day—I placed it on my vision board, and it all came true. Inside of myself, I had always been that fun-loving person, but I hadn't felt that I could act naturally until then. I went from the bullied teen to a D-list celebrity debutante within six months, and it only got better. The following three years at university were the best of my life. My time at Queen's was instrumental at helping me become comfortable with myself. I no longer wore the scar, hid who I was, or felt the need to create a persona. I stayed out as my authentic self, and I was accepted.

———

Just before graduating from Queen's in 2006, the students put on the annual Vogue Charity Fashion Show with proceeds going to local causes. The show creatively combined dance and runway elements, and it was sure to be exciting. Erin was one of the girls organizing the event. Because she knew I was a good dancer, she asked me to be in two of the dance sequences and to model underwear for the runway show. I took it as motivation to get in even better shape, so I agreed. A couple weeks before the show, Erin gave me the black boxer briefs I was going to wear.

Jokingly, I told Erin, "I think I should get giant angel wings and walk down the runway like in a Victoria's Secret show."

She teasingly replied, "Yeah, go for it." And so I did.

Two hours away in Ottawa, I found spectacular angel wings for rent in a costume store, and I decided to really make a statement before graduating. The night of the fashion show, I did two walks down the runway. The first was with a girl, Dana, wearing bridal lace, while I wore the fitted black boxer-briefs and a bowtie. Afterward, without forewarning Erin, I ran backstage and quickly changed into the giant angel wings and a G-string bikini and covered myself in glitter. I was incredibly nervous but intent on pushing the boundaries of this conservative university before I left. People accepted me, and I was comfortable with who I was, but I'd never been so brazen before. When it was time to take the stage, I walked to the end of the runway in what appeared to be bikini briefs and turned as if I were the queen of Queen's. The house went eerily silent as I revealed the thong and my bare, glittered cheeks—quiet enough to hear a pin drop—but I sighed with relief when an outburst of raucous laughter and applause followed. As I strutted backstage, the night I crawled through that window like a timid caterpillar in the mud came to mind, and here, just three years later, I had metamorphosed into a fabulous social butterfly.

4

Doctor Zhivago Jr.

After graduation, I returned to Egypt, keeping to my usual summer schedule. From there, I flew to Normandy to spend time with Grandfather, where I started to see gradual but consistent changes in him.

It wasn't like Grandfather to speak ill of people, but one evening, Dad and I were having dinner with him in the Hotel Barrière Le Royal restaurant when he became noticeably agitated. The light and comedic conversation about his friend changed course, and Grandfather began talking rudely about my mother, whom he hadn't seen in over ten years. His cold and bitter insults didn't make any sense, and neither of us understood how or why my mother had become the topic of Grandfather's agitation. There was no gray area about how deeply I loved Grandfather, but equally there was never going to be one with Mom. He was out of line, and I wasn't going to sit there and allow him to disrespect her. His discourse was entirely unwarranted, and I became upset—I don't recall ever using that tone with my grandfather before. My father abruptly put an end to the conversation in defense of Mom by instructing me to get up from the table and informing Grandfather we were leaving for Paris in the morning. Grandfather didn't appear to think he'd done anything wrong; in fact, he looked puzzled that we weren't amused. The oddest part was that it sounded as though he were talking about an entirely different person, not Mom. I appreciated and respected Dad for defending my mother, especially given that their divorce had been far from amicable, but I'd never seen Grandfather behave in that manner. That alone was concerning.

Later that evening, Dad and I were at the piano bar in the lobby; Grandfather had come to his senses and apologized. I didn't know if Dad had spoken to him about it or if he just felt bad about the things he'd said, but we ended up staying in Deauville with Grandfather for two more weeks. By the time I left France, Dad and I had become closer, but I had good reason to be worried about Grandfather. We all did.

———

It was the end of the first week of September, and I had three weeks before I was to begin a master's program at the London School of Economics. I wanted to spend that time with Mom and my family in Canada before heading across the pond for an extended period. Everything at home was the same as when I'd left. Like I had with my grandfather Omar, I'd observe Mom going through her morning routine and rituals. She began with opening each of the California shutters throughout the condominium, excluding my room. Then she'd brew her coffee, pour it into a white china cup, and load it with a ton of powdered Coffee-mate—which has convinced me that Mom doesn't even like coffee. She'd settle at the kitchen counter and hop on the phone, talking with one sibling after another, then Bubbie, and then her friends, all while picking at her pores with a pair of tweezers in a magnified mirror. When Mom unleashed her humor, she'd recount the funniest stories to each person as if telling them for the very first time. Her infectious laughter would surge beneath my door and reverberate in my bedroom. Sometimes I couldn't help but laugh at her comedy routines. If it was her day to go to the health club, she'd meet her friends and work out. Mom was lean, muscular, and in great shape, which is why we weren't prepared for the news that came on the last day of my first week home.

Mom woke up that morning and quietly headed out to her scheduled doctor's appointment. A few hours later, she called to inform me that she'd be at the clinic for a while longer than expected, and I sensed something was wrong. My mother normally communicated with color and energy, but this time her tone was glacial. She said, "They found something. They're going to do an ultrasound and biopsy."

I replied, "Okay, I don't understand," but she didn't tell me anything else.

"I'm coming," I said.

She quickly stated, "I need to call Anne," and then hung up.

Apparently, when Mom was at the health club with her friend Marlena, she'd told her that she felt something in her left breast. Marlena had urged her to go to the doctor, but Mom explained that she'd been a few months prior and had had a mammogram. Her friend cautioned that they might have missed something. I was grateful Mom responded to Marlena's warning by scheduling another appointment.

It wasn't long before Anne picked me up and drove me to the clinic where Mom was. By the time we arrived, Mom was wearing a powder-blue hospital gown and lying in bed. They had already completed the ultrasound and the technician was explaining the process for the biopsy. They were going to use a thin, hollow needle to remove tissue samples from the mass. The grueling part would be waiting two weeks for a final pathology report.

When the report finally came in after what seemed like two months, the doctor advised Mom to schedule an appointment with a surgeon and oncologist immediately because the ultrasound had shown something in her lymph nodes, too. He told us that, unfortunately, the lump wasn't benign and that Mom had stage two breast cancer, or worse.

Hearing the word *cancer* wasn't something to accept without difficulty. Just by looking at my mother, I knew she had barely begun to process the totality of it. Her eyes couldn't hide anything—she was scared. When she finally spoke, she asked, "I won't need chemo, will I? I won't lose my hair?" she asked, touching the side of her head.

"I'm not the oncologist, but the fact that it's showing up in your lymph nodes means that it has already spread." Mom was silent as he continued, "We see a mass on your thyroid, too, and we don't know if it's connected, but that's something we need to look into."

After a local anesthetic was administered, I headed outside to get some fresh air, leaving Mom with Anne. I didn't want Mom to see that I was worried, because it would upset her further. I had to be strong and methodical and focus on what needed to get done. With each step, I was processing everything and thinking out the logistics of canceling school and what needed to happen next. I walked to the end of the street and pulled my phone from my back pocket. Typically, when there was an urgent situation or crisis, I'd call Mom, but this time, I needed to call Dad.

I told Dad what the doctor had said while welling up with tears, and the first thing he asked was, "Did anyone say the word *metastatic*?"

I told him, "The doctor said it spread to the lymph nodes, but they don't know anything beyond that."

"Are you sure?"

"Yes, I'm sure." Then I heard a slight sigh of relief.

I explained to Dad that I wasn't going to London for my master's. I was determined to stay in Montreal to take care of Mom.

He agreed. "Stay in Montreal. We'll figure it out. Let me know if there's anything I can do."

I hung up and tilted my head up toward the sky to regroup before going back inside.

Dad was supportive, exactly what I needed at that moment; he always knew what to say, and he was sincere. Staying home for the surgery, her chemo treatments, and anything else Mom needed was something I wanted to do. Mom had done everything she could for me over the years, and I couldn't abandon her now. That wasn't an option.

I went back to the clinic and waited to hear what the next steps would be. When the doctor entered the room, Anne reached into her brown tote and pulled out a pen along with a dark green notebook. Anne began writing down everything the doctor said. She was a schoolteacher and knew her sister well. This wasn't my mother's first health scare, and Anne realized that Mom would have anxiety dealing with everything alone. At that point, none of us understood the treatment process, side effects, and risk factors, or knew about the palliative or supportive care she'd need. If we took notes, asked the right questions, and did research to familiarize ourselves with what it meant to have this disease, we could understand what it would take to survive it. This notebook became Mom's "Diary of Cancer."

Mom was understandably reticent on the ride home. When we arrived, she went straight to her computer and began researching anything she could find about breast cancer. Her face was drained of whatever joy had been there before her diagnosis and the sadness became profound—morbid. Whatever she read only increased her fear. While she was doing that, I sat down, composed an email to the university in London, and told them I would be deferring my enrollment for a year, but I didn't know if it would be possible to return at all. I received their reply later that afternoon affirming they would hold my spot. It was signed, "Best of luck." It felt impersonal, but they didn't know me. Not many people did.

Breast cancer had already caused loss and devastation in our family. Zadie's twin brother had a daughter, Sara, who like Mom had discovered a lump in her breast. She'd had surgery, but after having radiation, Sara made the decision to forgo chemo and took a holistic route instead. The results were unsuccessful—the cancer ate her alive. It was a cautionary tale for everyone in our family. Medical professionals also found that the BRCA2 gene runs in our family, a gene which predisposes women to breast or ovarian cancer and men to prostate and other types of cancer. To determine if we'd inherited the mutation, each of us had required testing. We had to consider the impact of this history on top of what Mom was dealing with, and it created more concern for everyone.

It wasn't surprising to see that Mom had a great support system from her entire family and bevy of friends. They were with us every step of the way, making sure Mom had everything she needed. Before the surgeon began treating her breast cancer, the surgeon removed the mass on Mom's thyroid so it wouldn't become cancerous. The surgeon couldn't tell us if a lumpectomy or a modified radical mastectomy was necessary for her breast until they went in. When they did, they cut the tumor out and kept cutting until the margins were clear and they'd gotten all the cells. They were able to perform a lumpectomy and remove the lymph nodes the cancer had spread to, but Mom's journey was just beginning.

The next step was to start chemotherapy. At first, the doctors weren't specific about whether three or six treatments were necessary. Had it been solely up to Mom, she wouldn't have had any. I don't think she was mentally prepared to lose her thick, beautiful blond hair, because it would be a constant reminder that she was sick. She asked her oncologist, "If you think everything was removed during the surgery, and I'm going to have radiation, why do I even need chemo?"

"No," I snapped. "I did not take a year off from school so you could not get fully better. We are doing the chemo *and* radiation and we're going to kill every last cancer cell." Chemotherapy wasn't optional, so she conceded. It was beautiful to see Aunt Anne, Uncle Holden, Uncle Simon, Aunt Natalie, Aunt Evelyn, Lisa, and everyone else, along with her closest friends, gathered together at her first chemotherapy session. They literally took over the treatment room. They sat there eating grape and cherry popsicles with Mom, while she told some of her funniest stories. She tried so hard to be the same, if only to make us feel that she'd be okay, but it was difficult to sustain for long.

It wasn't until her second treatment that Mom experienced the side effects and became really sick. It was difficult to watch her stumble into the bathroom clenching her stomach and then hunching over the sink to vomit. I couldn't control this part of the process, and it made me feel helpless. The only thing I could do was stand there, holding her hair back, asking her what she needed—and knowing the answer.

We received another dose of fear the night Mom was sitting on the sofa, lightly rubbing her scalp to relieve the burning sensation. When she slowly pulled her hands away from her head, clumps of hair clung between her fingers. The chemo was killing the cancer cells, but it was also destroying the healthy cells that cause hair growth. Her lips parted slightly and stayed open, as if she wanted to say something but couldn't. She became catatonic. Her pale cheeks stiffened, and the light in her eyes seemed to dim with each passing second. I scooped the hair out of her hands and threw it in the bathroom garbage can. I wouldn't be able to stop her long, beautiful hair from falling out, but at least she'd have control over how she lost the rest of it. I went back into the living room and grabbed Mom's hand, gently pulling her off the sofa. Without saying a word, I led her into the bathroom. I took out my clippers, wrapped a towel around her shoulders, and gently shaved her head.

While looking at my mother's reflection in the mirror, I couldn't help but recall the stories of Bubbie having her head shaved at Auschwitz. My mother suddenly looked gaunt, scared, and weak. She was now a prisoner of an illness that was trying to suck the life out of her.

The previous week, I'd taken her to the best stores in Montreal to help her find a selection of realistic-looking wigs. My mom had one condition when she'd agreed to undergo the chemotherapy—that it would be a secret. No one would know or could know that she was sick except a close selection of family and friends. Her cancer became her closet.

I was grateful when Mom finished each chemo treatment because it temporarily ended her nausea and vomiting. But there was more. The next step was giving Mom the prescribed injections for the following fourteen days in a row to boost her white blood cells and immune system so she wouldn't get sick. In the evening, I'd give Mom injections in a different place around her belly button because she couldn't bear to do it herself. When I'd gently pinch her skin to poke it with the needle, she'd cringe while looking away, the same way she'd turned away from the mirror when I shaved her hair off. When she was completely finished with chemotherapy, the radiation treatments began, held every weekday for nearly two months, burning her skin. To the eye, the deep redness appeared extremely uncomfortable. I knew she hated going. Her fatigue, stress, and bouts of depression grew worse. She had become fatalistic, and I could see that she'd all but given up hope.

I did everything possible to help Mom feel better and handle the breast cancer with a more positive outlook because I didn't want her to suffer in silence. All my efforts aside, I was incapable of removing or lessening her depression and fear of the unknown. In some ways, it triggered my anxiety. I understood there weren't any guarantees and that we had a five-year waiting period to see if the cancer would return. If it didn't, then Mom could begin to have her life back.

Taking care of Mom wasn't a problem; it was a choice. Dealing with everything without the ability to release the stress and worry it caused me—*that* was the problem. I worked hard to appear strong and confident, but I really wasn't. I put on a mask and just did my best to make it look that way—for her. Until the doctor said she was healthy again, the prospect of losing Mom was looming like distant thunder, murky shadows, and dark storm clouds.

I wasn't eating much; I'd lost weight, and I felt unhealthy both mentally and physically. My fight was not surrendering to the stress of everything past and present. Running and occasionally going out with friends from college brought temporary relief. Once I'd given Mom her injection, if she didn't need anything, I'd change clothes and go for a five- or six-mile run to try to clear my head. I didn't want to think about anything—not Mom, not death, not being alone, not cancer, not anything—I just ran. On one of those runs, I found myself on Anne's street. When I reached her house, I saw that Uncle Holden's car was parked out front. Simon and Evelyn's vehicles were in the driveway. All Mom's siblings were there, but Mom hadn't mentioned anything about them getting together. I jogged up to the front door and rang the doorbell. When Anne answered, I went inside to find them gathered in the living room, deep in conversation. Without interrupting, I took a seat, clasped my hands together and listened. They were discussing how best to take care of Mom and me should the worst-case scenario materialize. My eyes shifted downward to keep everyone from seeing the glassy layer of tears. Before I had processed the conversation, they transitioned to talking about the way they'd break the news to Bubbie, who had lost so many already. When Grandfather Zadie passed, it was the first time since the Holocaust that Bubbie had relived that deep suffering. They worried that Bubbie's fragile heart couldn't handle another loss.

My aunts and uncles sounded as if they had succumbed to the same fatalistic view as Mom. Perhaps I was naive, and they were pragmatic with their approach, but I wasn't prepared to yield to their thinking. I got up and went down the hall to the bathroom. As soon as I closed the door, the tears poured out. I turned on the faucet, cupped my hands together, and placed them under the cold water, over and over again, until the tears were washed from my eyes. When they stopped, I dropped to the floor and hunched over the toilet just in time. My fear and pain spewed out instead as vomit. Coughing and crying simultaneously, I stayed locked in that position until I'd purged everything. There was nothing left but dry heaves. After using toilet paper to wipe the residue from my mouth, I slowly pulled myself to my feet. Feeling completely hollow, I turned around to find Anne behind me. She pulled me close and held me until I stopped trembling. Moments later, Anne told me to wash the perspiration from my face, pull it together, and return home. She didn't want Mom to know that I was scared or what they were discussing. Even in that situation, I had to disguise my fear and act as if everything was going to be fine, the same way my aunts and uncles were doing. The difference was that I was going home to face Mom, and she was afraid.

Since I wasn't in school, there wasn't much to do. I was tired of being anxious, so I continued running, started working out at the gym again, and worked nights as a go-go dancer. Regardless of what I was doing, Mom remained my priority. Since I needed to better understand her illness, I volunteered three days a week with an organization called Hope & Cope that helped cancer patients. They provided enhanced knowledge of what my mother was going through, as well as the insight I needed to help care for her. At Hope & Cope, my job was to inform women about the services available at the hospital, and in return, they helped me learn what the illness had taken from them. For nine months, I worked with women who were

courageously fighting breast cancer. More often than not, I was the
first person they saw after their diagnosis. Many of them confessed
that they rarely cried in front of their doctor. But when they were
sitting with me, learning how to apply eyeliner to make it seem like
they hadn't lost all their eyelashes or eyebrows, reality hit and they
lost their stoicism. I told them where they could buy or acquire wigs
and other things they hadn't needed to know about until then. Some
of these women won their battles, while others passed away—but
they were all fighters. In some capacity, each of those brave women
helped me become a better caregiver for my mother. When Mom finally completed all her treatments, I told her she was a survivor—just
like Bubbie. The problem was that *I* was barely surviving. I didn't
know what was to come, but I just couldn't handle any more internal
pain or conflict. I was frozen in hell.

5

Che! (Oy Vey)

In Montreal I was wary everywhere I went. Being home caused my longstanding stress to return, especially after having freedom, friends, and room to breathe at Queen's University. I was suffocating on the toxicity of hatred, choking on prejudice, and distressed by the possibility that death was waiting. I felt broken.

A few months had passed, and I'd spent the majority of that time with Mom or at the hospital. That year marked the first Christmas I hadn't gone to Egypt to be with Dad or to France to spend time with Grandfather. During the winter months, darkness descends early in Montreal, and the snow blankets Quebec's landscape with endless layers. I wanted the ruthless, penetrating cold to cut through me and freeze the sadness, fear, and isolation growing inside. I couldn't tell anyone what I needed and what I was feeling. I had stayed home to take care of my mother, not to have people feel sorry for me or to make things more stressful. My time at home wasn't about me, so I continued to do my best by trying to avoid the triggers that made me feel worse.

Graduating from Queen's helped me advance to another level in my life, and it was somewhat liberating—I wasn't the same. My feet moved steadily toward the boundary between shadow and light, even in Montreal. The students from university who lived in Montreal only knew me as Junior. They didn't know the bullied and picked-on kid from elementary and high school, which made it more enjoyable to go out. Interacting with people outside our home and the hospital made me feel that I was still myself and that I was beginning to belong.

I had always enjoyed dancing, but now I used it as therapy, too. Working as a go-go dancer or party animator made people more familiar with me around town, and I made friends because of it. Following a party or event with my fellow dancers Gill, Alyssa, and Lisa, we'd meet other friends at the popular Wunderbar in the W Montreal hotel on weekends. I'd slide in the back seat of my car, quickly change out of the red jumpsuit I danced in, and head into the hotel lounge to enjoy the evening with them. The music had a way of making me feel more alive than when I woke up in the morning; the energy became something I craved.

One Saturday, I spotted a petite brunette from high school sitting at the bar, twirling her drink with a cocktail straw while bobbing her head to a house mix that reminded me of my summer in Mykonos. When our eyes met, she flagged me over. Trying to minimize the shock on my face, I headed in her direction. Julia was a couple of years older than me, but she was one of the few people who had been kind to me in high school. She was sitting next to Gabriel, her hairstylist. His profession was to keep women looking fabulous. The rumor was that Gabriel was in such high demand that his well-known and affluent clients kept him on speed dial. Julia didn't waste time introducing me to her friend, although I already knew who he was, and I'd heard he'd be at the W that night. He was one of the reasons the W was a hot spot.

Gabriel was part Latin with thick black hair, perfect scruff, and beautiful white teeth that looked like Chiclets—like a modern-day Che Guevara. His tight black V-neck T-shirt revealed some cool tattoos on his arms, along with an impressive white-gold Cartier watch and dozens of braided, beaded, and brilliant bracelets. He was a classic bad boy, but fashionable, whereas my style was definitely casual; I wore sweatpants and a hoodie almost everywhere I went and not much else.

I never thought I'd be able to date a guy like Gabriel, but he was one to hope for, and I did. That night, with blaring music, smiles, and cocktails, Julia filled me with something I didn't have when it came to guys—confidence. After years of bullying, I still hadn't developed high self-esteem, especially when it came to men. I listened to her vouch for my character with a glowing report, surprised that anyone in high school had noticed me to that extent. As soon as Julia told Gabriel I was a nice guy, I was certain I didn't have a chance with him. I thought Gabriel must like other bad boys. His vibe was mischievous, and his intoxicating eyes had something more intense behind them. I didn't believe that it was anything more than an introduction, but it was nice. Before leaving them, I inadvertently suggested Gabriel and I catch a movie some time. He paused, letting his eyes glide down my body, lingering just below my waist long enough to tease me before he smiled slyly and replied, "That sounds fun." We exchanged numbers, and I made my way to the dance floor to escape everything else and hope for something new.

A few days later, I was leaving the hospital when Gabriel called me.

"Is that offer still good?" he questioned.

"What?"

"The movie. Or were you just—"

"No. I mean, yeah," I said, sounding surprised.

"When are we going?" he asked.

"I don't know."

"Tonight?"

"Yeah, that works. I have something to do, but we can go out after."

"Should I pick you up?"

"No. Text me your address and I'll swing by and get you."

That something was dinner with Mom and her nightly injection, and I wasn't going to miss it.

Mom and I had a nice dinner, but the conversation was light that evening. She hadn't returned to her usual self, but I knew she appreciated our time together. I missed her radiant smile and lively, jovial demeanor. When we got home, I made sure she had everything she needed before letting her know I was going to a movie with a friend.

I drove to Gabriel's place and picked him up because I wanted to take him to the Guzzo cinema in Saint-Laurent for privacy. I was still cautious about who I was seen with, and the Guzzo was outside of where I lived and normally hung out.

Gabriel seemed excited and more talkative than when we met. He filled me in on what was happening around town and gave me updates on a few of his local celebrity clients. He was up on everything because of the conversations that took place in his busy salon.

When I glanced over at him, he had an inquisitive look on his face as he watched me maneuver the stick shift. I took Gabriel's left hand, bearing the signature watch clasped around his wrist, and placed it on top of mine. Gently intertwining our fingertips, I continued working the stick. Gabriel seemed to enjoy the ride. When we arrived at the theater, I bought the tickets, and we went inside. Even with the theater less than half full, we strategically isolated ourselves. He followed me up the stairs to the last row just as the movie was beginning. Ninety minutes later the credits began rolling. I was so distracted by how good it felt sitting next to Gabriel that I couldn't recall anything about the movie.

Although I'd gone on a date with Gabriel, it didn't change anything. I wasn't the smooth playboy my grandfather was. Other than Donnie, who'd threatened to kill me, and the guys in Mykonos who were just having summer flings, I didn't have second dates, so Gabriel caught me off guard when he called and asked me to have dinner with him a week later. Responding coolly to his invite, I accepted. When I hung up the phone, my head was swirling with excitement, but I wasn't sure what Gabriel saw in me. I wasn't out, popular, or in the best physical shape. I still had good muscle definition, but since I'd been taking care of Mom rather than myself, I'd skipped parts of my usual self-care regimen.

I went into the living room to check on Mom. The glare from the television was all that illuminated the room. She was sitting on the sofa, staring blankly at it. I grabbed one of the fleece blankets out of the hall closet and draped it softly across her. As soon as I sat next to her, her head fell on my shoulder and she held my hand until she drifted off to sleep. My love for my mother was so great—and hers for me—that I was unable to release my fear of losing her. Although she didn't know everything about me, she loved me. I was depleted, scared, and hurting.

I was glad I'd met Gabriel because I needed someone to be there for me the way I was for Mom. Gabriel fit into my world so easily that I grasped onto him like a lifeline. He was the distraction I needed—available, kind, and fun—and he didn't pull a gun on me.

Other than Bubbie and Zadie's marriage, I'd been surrounded by several failed marriages and relationships. Dad had been married three times by that point. Mom had multiple failed relationships and was single. And as for Grandfather, he'd only married once but kept company with numerous women. I didn't want to be like that or make the same mistakes. After our first two dates had gone well, I started to think that Gabriel could be the one to last a lifetime. Gabriel was from my home city and we happened to revolve around the same network of people. Some of my friends were engaged, others married, and several of them already had kids. I, too, wanted a monogamous relationship with the right person. I wanted to experience love, happiness, and acceptance.

When I wasn't with Mom, Gabriel and I spent a great deal of time together, and it didn't take long before we became more serious. Every couple of nights, I'd make up an excuse to get out of the house just so I could watch a movie or hang out with him. Then it became daily. Dating Gabriel felt revolutionary.

I appreciated how open Gabriel was when he'd talk about his family, friends, career—his life in general. He'd say and do whatever he wanted, and he didn't seem to care what anyone thought. He had incredible taste, and I was learning more about style and fashion just by being around him. Before I met him, I didn't care about clothes or cars. I always had what I needed, and that was more than enough.

I didn't want material things because, frankly, I didn't care for them, but Gabriel was materialistic, and his cravings began to rub off on me. His impressive watch collection drew me closer to his lifestyle. Before long, I wanted one, too, and I found myself trying to keep up with his taste. When I was out shopping with Mom, she'd catch me eyeing watches in display cases. She probably assumed the sudden interest came from being around Grandfather and his friends.

I was generous with Gabriel because I wanted him to be happy—and because I thought he was out of my league. If he mentioned something that he wanted, I'd buy it for him. Although it happened less frequently, I thought it was nice that he'd buy me gifts, too. When Gabriel and I met, I was twenty-two, and he was a few years older. Gabriel wasn't formally educated, but he was well-traveled, cultured, and he didn't have to hide me from his family or friends. His mom and sister knew and accepted that Gabriel was gay. When he took me to meet them, his sister jokingly asked me, "What do you even see in him?" It was the freedom.

Gabriel was a mystery, and there were times I sensed he was lost and hiding his truth or secrets—whatever they were. I was patient because I believed time would expose them. Our time alone was intense yet comforting. Gabriel became an immediate distraction from my stress, and he was beginning to make a difference in the way I handled my mother's anxiety.

I wasn't sure what to think when Gabriel invited me to his family's estate in the Laurentian Mountains. We'd only been hanging out for eight weeks, but I wanted to experience what it would be like to have that kind of time alone with him. Sneaking around, sitting in a dark theater, or pretending we were friends in public was not my idea of building a relationship, certainly not a healthy one. Grandfather didn't hide his relationships; he was who he was. I wanted to be true to who I was, so I took the opportunity to feel normal, if only for a day or two.

The next afternoon, Gabriel and I drove the scenic route to the mountains. When I glanced in my rearview mirror, I saw the world I left behind as I entered another—just as I had in Mykonos. His family's cottage was located near the top of a mountain and the view from the driveway was strikingly beautiful. When we went inside, I thought I'd walked through the doors of a Ralph Lauren showroom. While I was admiring the decor, Gabriel was placing wood logs in the imposing fireplace. He grabbed a few pages of newspaper next to the cabinet, crumpled them up, and shoved them beneath the logs. Then he picked up a small box of matches from the mantle, crouched down, and struck one, delicately placing it against the newspaper. When the flame caught, it quickly spread to the dry wood, and in moments the fire crackled and burned with passionate fury. The room was aglow. Floating sparks trailed up the chimney to the sound of Gabriel's applause. He spun toward me playfully and reached for my hand.

"Look at this view," he said.

"I know. I—" Gabriel placed his finger against my lips and kissed me.

Blanketed with thick snow, the mountains were breathtaking. Everything was perfect and still. Holding my hand, he led me downstairs, opened a closet, and looked at my feet. Gabriel handed me a pair of snowshoes and said, "Let's take a sunset walk." I observed Gabriel take in the crisp air as if he needed it to live. He was more relaxed than I'd ever seen him before. We took in the view while walking along a trail that led to an overlook of a beautiful lake. He pointed out the mountains he used to ski and told me about his favorite restaurants in the towns neatly nestled nearby. A half hour later, we went back inside, removed our coats and shoes, and returned to the living room. Gabriel disappeared. When he returned, he had two glasses and a bottle of wine that we shared in front of the fire. For the first time, with only the glow of the fire lighting our faces, Gabriel said, "I love you." And I loved him, too.

Our time together was uninterrupted, and it was the first time I'd spent the entire night wrapped in Gabriel's arms. The next morning, he made me breakfast, and after a late morning walk, I told him I needed to get back to Mom; she thought I was up north with Gill.

Given all the turmoil and uncertainty, it felt like being with Gabriel was the safest place for me, but the more I got to know him, the less I was convinced. He was good for me during that time, and really good in bed, but he wasn't as caring as I'd hoped for. Other than an occasional "How's your mom?" he didn't show genuine interest. I didn't want to drag my worries into that relationship, so I made a mental note and let it go. I needed to enjoy being happy—and marvel in what felt like my first love.

Every so often, I'd run into some of the mothers of the kids who'd bullied me. They'd see me doing charity work at the hospital or helping others in some capacity. Unlike their kids, the moms were always nice to me. They'd stop and talk to me, ask how I was doing, or go out of their way to say hello. After I'd been with Gabriel for a few months, one of those mothers came up to me and said, "I heard you're dating my hairstylist. I told him that if he hurts you, he'd be done in this town." I didn't realize how much people knew about me or that they even cared, but it made me wonder how much my family actually knew.

It was already March, and I'd been sneaking around with Gabriel for a couple of months. I was tired of the lies, of hiding and making excuses. I wanted the kind of support Gabriel had from his mom. It was time to come out to Mom. If I wanted my three worlds to merge into one, I needed to be honest so I could be comfortable as myself. Honesty and authenticity are inextricably linked. I wanted Mom to know about Gabriel, but more importantly, I wanted my mother to know the truth about her son.

I'd already met Gabriel's family, and I wanted him to meet my mother. Besides, people were starting to hear that I was dating him. I was scared but resolved to tell Mom. I was concerned about the way Dad would take it, too, but for now I decided to address one world, and one parent, at a time. As for Mom, I hoped she could get through it. I needed my mother to be accepting of me. It would kill me if she saw me the way she saw others in my community. We weren't freaks. Maybe this reality would help her see us all differently.

When I walked into the apartment that afternoon, Mom was sitting at the kitchen counter flipping through her day-planner and writing notes. She seemed agitated, and I assumed she wasn't feeling well. A few minutes later, she put the pen down and looked at me as though she already knew something.

"Where were you last night?" she asked, flipping the hair of her wig off her shoulder.

"I was with Gabriel."

"And he is?"

"Someone I'm dating," I said, finally telling the truth.

Mom closed her planner, and the tension grew.

"This—this is going to kill Bubbie! She's too old to hear this!"

"She survived the Nazis, and this is going to kill her?"

"You're going to kill me—I'm sick! Don't you care?"

"Mom, please!"

I tried to look away. I couldn't let her see what she was doing to me.

"And don't tell your father! Don't tell anyone! God help you if your father or the rest of Egypt finds out. You've always caused me stress. That's probably how I got this—"

"No! No! I'm the nurse! I'm not the one who made you sick. I'm the one who's always taken care of you."

She snatched her planner from the counter and looked at me as if she had failed me as a mother. She shook her head and walked toward her bedroom, seething.

"This is why I couldn't tell you," I called after her, but she didn't respond. She closed the door to her room.

After all those years of hiding, my biggest fears had come true. The reason I hadn't come out was that there was only one person I needed to accept me, and the moment I finally had the courage to tell her, she didn't. My mother had always been my biggest advocate and protector. She claimed to love me unconditionally, and I had believed her. I always did everything I could for her, but when I told her my truth, none of it mattered. This was the red line, and she withdrew her love and acceptance. I wasn't just disappointed in Mom, but in humanity, and in that moment, I had nothing left I wanted to say. In the same way I had as a bullied kid with suicidal thoughts, I curled into a fetal position on the sofa and tried to sleep through it. That was my way of dealing with pain. Some call it depression.

Mom and I existed in uncomfortable silence for a few weeks. She went through her routine without speaking to me, and I didn't say anything to her. It was hurtful, but I'd said everything that was nec-essary. I'd finally shared the one significant thing that gave me freedom from hiding, lying, and feeling less than human. I wanted to believe that if my mother accepted me, it wouldn't matter if others didn't.

At some point, Mom must have told Anne, because she came over and worked to rebuild the bridge, but it wasn't easy. It wasn't what Mom wanted, so I figured it wouldn't hurt her if I told her another truth. "There are two arguments for people being gay: nature or nurture. Either way, it's *your* fault. It's either how you raised me or it's the genetics you gave me," I told her. She retorted with something about the likelihood that I'd get AIDS and die, assuring me that only a lifetime of hardship, loneliness, and misery awaited me. "Just get married and have kids—be normal!" she said.

I was devastated, yet Mom was the one who was grieving—as though some nonexistent straight son was dead, and she was left with me. Her response didn't change who I was or how I felt; it just sucked the air out of my lungs, and in that moment, I thought maybe if I had killed myself way back when, it would have been easier for her than this.

———

After a few months of dating, things began to change with Gabriel. He went to Mexico with friends, and when he returned, he was different. We became less physical and slightly less communicative. Since Gabriel was the first person I had truly dated and loved, I wasn't ready to lose him, especially after it seemed I'd lost Mom. I tried to get his attention by working out more. I bought him gifts regularly and worked to keep up conversation between us, but he wasn't responding. I didn't know how to deal with it when Gabriel began withdrawing a little at a time, so I was persistent in finding other ways to keep his attention.

I went to see my cousin Lisa in May and asked her to borrow a thousand dollars so I could take Gabriel to the Turks and Caicos Islands, thinking it would make things better between us. At first, he was excited about going, and then, the night before we were to leave, Gabriel called me and said, "I don't think we should go. I think it's over."

"What's wrong?" I asked dismissively.

"It's not you, it's me. I'm—I'm a mess, Omar," he replied flatly.

"No, you're not," I insisted. "You're just stressed or something. That's why you need this vacation. Let's just go. We'll have a good time and things will get better."

Gabriel kept talking, but I wasn't hearing him, largely because I wasn't prepared to accept what he had to say. I knew something was going on with him, and it wasn't good, but it didn't have anything to do with me. I didn't want to tell people we hadn't gone on the trip that I had paid for. Besides, I was committed to making it work between us. After a round of convincing, Gabriel agreed, and we went on the trip.

Turks and Caicos should have ignited something in Gabriel. The clear waters, powder-white sand beaches, magnificent restaurants, and exciting nightlife offered a perfect romantic vacation for us. But the sweeping views and incredible backdrop didn't change him. As soon as we hit the beach, I could tell by his behavior that I'd wasted my time. He stared at the ocean as if he were somewhere without me. Gabriel had told me how he felt, but my heart felt something different.

A few hours later, we went back to our room to change for dinner. We had plans to go to a nightclub that evening. I was hopeful the energy in the club would lift his spirits, and we'd have fun dancing and laughing the way we had before he'd gone to Mexico. While I was deciding what to wear, Gabriel took off his clothes, flung them over a chair, and went to take a shower. A small plastic bag with white powder dropped out of his shorts pocket onto the floor next to his shoes. I bent down and picked it up. My mouth fell open while I waited for my thoughts to catch up. My family had raised me to be against drugs, and until now, I'd never seen cocaine. Instantly, everything made sense. I wasn't surprised that Gabriel used. He was the cool, former model guy that had his own collection of secrets. I hadn't seen them, because I wasn't ready to accept them. With him, everything needed to be fast and fun. When it wasn't, he'd move on and just let whatever it was go. It was clear to me his behavior wasn't the same, but I still didn't want to believe cocaine was the only cause.

When I heard the shower shut off, I contemplated putting the cocaine back on the floor, pretending not to have seen it. I decided it wasn't the time or place to tell Gabriel what I wanted to say, because it would make things worse. But I had to say something; I needed to see his reaction. I sat waiting on the edge of the bed, trying to look unfazed by my discovery. Gabriel came out of the bathroom with a thick, white towel wrapped around his waist and saw his packet of cocaine hanging between my fingers.

"What's this?" I asked.

"Now you're going through my things?" he said, sounding suddenly defensive.

"Of course not. But should I?"

"I don't know. Maybe."

"This fell out of your pocket, and I picked it up," I replied. "So, what is it?"

"What does it look like?" he said, removing his towel.

"I didn't know you did blow."

"Is that a problem for you?" he said, waiting for my reaction.

"No," I said, trying to sound cool. "I was wondering why you didn't offer me any," I lied.

Gabriel shrugged. "Really? You're not the type."

"Where'd you get it?" I questioned, to forestall him asking if I wanted to try it.

"Here, at the resort."

"You know someone here?"

"No. It's everywhere. It's easy to get."

"Okay. But why?" I asked naively.

He slipped into a pair of pale-blue boxer briefs and sat in the chair across from me. He lowered his head into his hands, as if he wanted to confess something. Gabriel closed his eyes and took a deep breath before he began. That night, he opened up and shared more about his life. It was difficult to determine if he was making excuses for using or if he was involved in something more sinister. Maybe he was hoping to scare me away with the story about his stepfather's role in an organized crime ring. After what I heard, I couldn't tell if he was lying.

I let him use his cocaine out in the open for the rest of the trip. I even kept it in my pocket when he wore his Speedo to the beach. After watching him snort it, I knew it was more than recreational. The personal things Gabriel shared about himself and his family didn't change anything between us, but they allowed me to admit to myself that maybe Gabriel wasn't who I thought he was—or who I wanted him to be. The hole in my heart grew deeper, and the saddest part was that I still wanted him, as he was. Later, I even considered not going to London for my master's just so I could be with him. Since I'd always been a caregiver, I thought maybe it was possible I could help him, too.

On the way home, we had a stop in Miami. For whatever reason, security flagged my bags for additional drug enforcement screening. I spotted Gabriel leisurely walking away toward a bench, disconnecting himself from what was happening. No one would have thought we were together—I felt like I was throwing my life away for someone who maybe didn't care as much about me as I did for them. Sitting in a room by myself while they rummaged through my belongings was infuriating. I didn't know if there were traces of cocaine on my things or what would happen if there were. After they cleared my luggage, Gabriel never apologized, took responsibility, or mentioned anything about it.

We made it back to Montreal without further incident. Although things weren't any better with Mom, all I wanted to do was go home. When I dropped Gabriel off at his place, he grabbed his suitcase from the trunk and gave me a kiss on the cheek. When I got home, I sent him a message telling him I was glad we survived the trip.

The next day, I called Gabriel, but he didn't respond. I went to his house to check on him, but he wasn't there. A week later, Gabriel ended things between us by sending me a text. Emotionally, I was a mess; my heart was broken, and it wasn't solely because of him. I'd given almost everything I had to my mother, and Gabriel got everything that was left. I didn't want to end up divorced or alone like my parents, so I'd poured my heart and soul into that relationship. I wanted to be with someone capable of loving and appreciating me as I was, and I believed he did. Gabriel was my first *I love you* and he was the one to say it first, which made the breakup even harder. I never knew a pain so deep or cutting. I didn't have Mom to lean on, so I kept the pain—from both of them—to myself. I went through each day as though everything were fine from the outside, but on the inside, I was utterly destroyed.

A week later, Gabriel called and said, "I'm sorry I haven't been in touch. It's not you. You haven't done anything. It's me. Like I told you before, I'm not in a good place—and I just wanted you to know that."

"Okay," was all I needed to say.

Gabriel had gone from someone I'd seen every day to someone I never saw again. As soon as I hung up, it hit me all over again, and somehow, I felt even worse. Subconsciously, maybe I'd hoped he was calling to apologize and get back together. I couldn't call Dad, because he still didn't know I was gay, and Mom still hadn't accepted me. Her entire side of the family knew, and they were aware that I was dating Gabriel. They never said anything about it or treated me any differently, so I grabbed my car keys and headed out. I was certain I could talk to my cousin Jessica.

I parked in front of Anne's house and ran up to the front door, banging on it as if their house were on fire. Anne opened the door, and I could tell by her eyes that she detected the sadness on my face. Neither of us said anything. She stepped aside and let me in as if she knew something terrible had happened. I hurried past her, quickly climbed the flight of stairs, ran past the computer station, and knocked on Jessica's white bedroom door. As soon as she answered, I saw her flushed eyes and beautiful face stained with tears. Anne probably thought I was there to comfort Jessica, but what I needed was for Jessica to console me.

Jessica was a year younger than me, and she had always treated me well. She had thick, brown hair, dark brown eyes, and an oval-shaped face. She reminded me of Sandra Bullock. Her baby sister, Zoe, resembled Anne Hathaway. They are both beautiful girls and genuinely sweet.

I shut the door and grabbed Jessica's hand. "What's wrong?" I asked.

"I just broke up with Zach," she whimpered.

I broke down and started crying. Jessica wiped her puffy eyes with her hands and studied my face. She knew I wasn't crying over Zach, because—why would I?

"Omie, what is it?"

"Gabriel broke up with me."

Jessica's whimpers became loud, heaving sobs. She wrapped her arms around me until that wave of sadness was flushed out. When we plopped down on her bed, I was emotionally drained. Jessica positioned herself against the headboard; I leaned against the footboard, and we faced the window overlooking the backyard with tears rolling down our cheeks. The swing set and tree house that we played in as kids was still there—only we had changed. I wished life were that simple again, the way it had been when I was young, before the bullying began, before I knew I was gay, before Mom's cancer, before Mom rejected me, and before Gabriel broke my heart. After a momentary silence, Jessica and I locked eyes and burst into laughter, grasping the absurdity of our despondency. Our mirth transitioned into drenching tears, a short pause, heaving sobs, and then back to explosive laughter. That's when I realized how close those two emotions actually were. From then on, laughter became my coping mechanism. Whenever I had to deal with anything difficult or stressful, I simply made a punch line or joke of it. The relief from laughter was much stronger than the tears from sadness.

Followed by a quick tap on Jessica's door, Anne entered the room before Jessica could reply. Our heart-rending wails followed by bouts of hysterical laughter had drifted downstairs. Anne's expression told us that she didn't know what to make of the situation.

"What happened?" Anne asked. She looked at Jessica first, and then her eyes turned to me when Jessica didn't reply. "We," I said, pointing at Jessica and then myself, "we were both dumped today."

Anne's expression shifted from worried to pensive.

"Are you okay?" she asked, glancing at the two of us.

Jessica and I nodded, and then I confessed, "We're just laughing and crying our way through it."

Anne nodded approvingly.

"Losing the first person you love is really hard, but you'll survive," she assured us. She asked if we needed anything, and when we shook our heads, Anne left the room, gently closing the door behind her.

Twenty minutes later, Anne returned to tell me Mom was there to pick me up. She must have told Mom what had happened because I didn't need a ride. I gave Jessica a big hug and went downstairs to find Mom waiting for me at the foot of the stairs.

"You broke up with Gabriel?"

"Yeah."

"Are you upset?" she asked.

"I was," I replied, shrugging off her concern.

Since Gabriel and I had returned from Turks and Caicos, I'd been going through the grieving process. That day was the end of it. That evening and that relationship ended in laughter.

"There will always be more—put your losses behind you. He might have been your first, but he won't be your last boyfriend," Mom told me.

It didn't escape my notice that she'd said *boyfriend*.

When we left Anne's house, I headed to my car.

"Follow me," Mom insisted.

"Where are we going?"

"There's one thing that always makes me feel better," she said, before closing her car door.

I followed Mom from Anne's house through the streets of downtown Montreal. She pulled into a parking lot next to the Château d'Ivoire, one of the finest jewelry stores in town. I parked alongside of her and walked behind her into the building.

"This is something I've been meaning to do for you," she said. "I know you've wanted a nice watch because I've seen you looking at them. I want to get you one as a graduation gift and to thank you for taking the year off school for me. Today won't be the day you got dumped, but the day you got that timepiece you've wanted," she said, tapping on the glass case with a Bulgari watch right below her index finger.

The watch was Mom's way of saying she understood my pain. She'd been through the heartache of breakups and a divorce, which allowed her to identify with the feelings I had for Gabriel. Human emotions are neither gay nor straight, and this was her unique way of showing that she finally accepted me.

From that day on, I was resolved not to let anyone else or any other boyfriend enter my heart until I could fully love myself. I closed off my heart to outside influences while I worked to accept, appreciate, and love the most important relationship in my life, the one with someone I was just beginning to know, the one with me. Until then, I would allow no other relationship to take precedence. If I wasn't learning or growing and receiving an equal amount of love as I was giving, I would end that relationship immediately. And when it would end, I'd just laugh it off—and then buy myself something nice.

I waited so long to have that first boyfriend, and I'd hoped it would last forever; but nothing lasts forever. It was the end of my degree at Queen's University, of my first relationship, of Mom's illness, of her not accepting me, and of my life in Montreal. It was a time of closure and new beginnings.

6

New Beginnings

In June, I returned to my aristocratic home in Egypt. I was back on my usual schedule of time with Dad, Karem, and Faten before two weeks in France with Grandfather. That summer, I was more popular than I'd ever been. I think people sensed I was freer and lighter than ever before. I attributed it to the fact that Mom, Uncle Holden, Aunt Anne, Aunt Natalie, Uncle Simon, Aunt Evelyn, Lisa, Jessica, Mikey and that entire side of my family knew I was gay. Their acceptance had given me peace and closure. Now, I only had two worlds.

The deferral of my master's was a bit of a blessing because two of my best friends from Queen's University were going to be joining me at the London School of Economics. Not only was I moving to London that October—I was going to be living with Raphael, who had played for the lacrosse team, and Sara. Raph and I had traveled together during spring break every year since we met, and we were practically brothers by that point. Even our parents became friends. It didn't take long for me to settle in London and acclimate to the program at LSE. It had a worldwide academic reputation, and I loved being in London. It was closer to Egypt, which made it easier to see my family and spend time with my little brother on holiday weekends. When I had time off from university, I met them in Rome, Paris, or Madrid, and went home to Egypt two additional times that year.

To better adapt and meet people in London, I made a standing reservation for myself at Nobu, a Japanese restaurant in Berkeley Square, every Friday night. I'd just sit at the bar and talk to people. I quickly discovered that I had a unique ability to connect. After two weeks, I became friends with people from the upper echelons of London society, which was based on prestige, respect, and old money. Because of my grandfather, I could get into any private club I wanted—including Annabel's, where aristocrats, tycoons, and royals like Princess Diana used to party.

Dad and Grandmother were proud that I'd been accepted to LSE and gave me money each month for rent, living, and tuition. As far back as I could recall, Grandmother Faten had wanted me to become a banker, a lawyer, or a doctor—anything but an actor. Since they were paying all my bills in London, I could just focus on school and enjoy life. I lived on a nearly unlimited budget, with access to all the greatest nightclubs, museums, and events. My first week there, I went into the Royal Opera House and bought tickets for the entire opera and ballet seasons. Almost every day, after school or on my lunch break, I'd go to the last-minute ticket kiosks and buy day-of tickets to see a musical or a play. Often, I went by myself. I enjoyed being alone and merely social. Naturally, there were occasions when I invited people to go with me, but I didn't date, nor did I try to. I just appreciated exploring the culture and the city, developing friendships, and going to as many events as I could. This was a year of personal edification, of being selfish and spoiled. I felt like I'd been taking care of everyone, and I needed to put that on hold. London meant total freedom, so I claimed it and continued finding myself.

Queen's had been a period of change, but London was a time of significant transformation. While Gabriel and I never spoke again, his fashion influence remained strong. I couldn't avoid the allure of the West End boutiques or the famed shops on Bond Street. The most exclusive brands, designer fashion, fine jewelry, and luxury goods were laid at my feet, making it easy for me to spend a small fortune. As I now cared about my image, I wore the beautiful clothing I bought to my standing reservations at Nobu. I spent years carefully observing Grandfather connect and interact with anyone he wanted. I'd studied him sitting at the piano in the lobby of the hotel he frequented most often. It was how he drew people in. He was finely dressed and as classy as ever. His singing wasn't the best, but it didn't matter, because it was authentic. He attracted the attention of the most beautiful women, and then he'd invite them to dinner that evening. Sometimes they became brief affairs, and others were just companions. When he didn't want to be alone, he wasn't.

Maybe Grandfather had it right, and I'd had it wrong all along. Maybe true companionship couldn't come from one person, especially for someone who lives in multiple worlds, and during my time in London I found that friends are for friendship, lovers for love, and family for fulfillment. I'd studied Grandfather so much over the years that, unconsciously, I'd taken on some of his mannerisms and cultivated a handful of the same instincts. With little effort, I'd connect with the most fascinating, beautiful people. Often, it was a fabulously dressed woman who was alone. Like Grandfather, I'd meet my dinner date at the bar downstairs at Nobu and invite him or her to have dinner with me or go to the theater just for companionship.

Natasha was one of the women I met at Nobu. She was intelligent, charming, crafty, sexual, and seductively beautiful. Within minutes, I found out that she worked for a hedge fund. She began to travel everywhere with me, and even met Grandmother Faten in Cairo, who was convinced I was dating a high-class hooker, although Natasha obviously wasn't. She was, however, outrageously wild and adventurous—like me. Natasha lived life to the fullest and disregarded the repercussions. Our subsequent travels led to many sordid adventures, which helped to free the parts of my personality and sexuality I had repressed in an attempt to always be proper.

The more I learned who I was, the more I mirrored Grandfather. There were moments when I thought about certain aspects of his life and then considered my own. I'd smile because it felt like *The Tale of Two Omars*. Like Grandfather, I loved culture, art, and museums. Admiring and appreciating life, I'd frequently walk along the banks of the Thames and across the London Millennium Footbridge, stroll past the Globe, and head to the Tate Modern, where I'd sit on a bench and study or read.

That year was expansive. Having Raph at LSE was like having a piece of Queen's with me, and that meant the world to me. Queen's was where my confidence had evolved, and Raph accepted the real me. He was a constant reminder that it was okay for me to be who I was while doing what I loved. Raph was my straight friend, the athlete, the jock, and the superstar from Queen's. He'd traveled with Dad and me to Paris and Barcelona that year and helped build the bridge between my world at Queen's and the Egyptian side of my family, allowing me to be more myself. Raph helped me connect the separate worlds like a Venn diagram. All three worlds were beginning to exist together and not on the peripheries of one another. The circles kept moving inward, and I hoped that one day they might become concentric. I wanted to live in one world with one me, one Omar.

The summer before I returned to Egypt to write my thesis and take up residence, Raph, Sara, Graham, and a few other friends decided to spend two weeks in Israel and Palestine. I hadn't been to Israel since my high school trip and decided to join. Our plans were to go to Tel Aviv, rent a house, sit on the beach, spend a day in Jerusalem, and go to the Dead Sea. Gill even flew in to join us, and I showed her around London then took her to Bath and Stonehenge before leaving for Israel. At the airport, security was set up outside of the ticketing area for prescreening. They saw the name on my passport and flagged me. I didn't think much about it, because they screen the flights to Israel well, but I wanted to show my friends that it was okay, so I spoke to security in fluent Hebrew. But because of my Arabic name, speaking Hebrew made security come the conclusion that I must be Hamas or Hezbollah. Throughout the airport, security followed us around. A guy using a newspaper to shield his face tailed us everywhere we went. He was so busy following me that he didn't notice his paper was upside down; it was like a bad spy novel. When I reached my gate, security told me that I couldn't wait with the other passengers; I had to wait underground, under the tarmac. They made Raph go with me because they saw a guy with an Arabic name and a Frenchman traveling together, and probably assumed we were headed to Israel to engage in some unknown terrorist activity. They went through all our bags and strip searched us, swiping handheld metal detector paddles between our butt cheeks.

Despite our experience at the airport, when we arrived, we had the most amazing time, filled with parties, beach adventures, and touring. I fell so in love with the land, the people, and the region that I decided to change the subject of my thesis at the last minute to conflict resolution in the Middle East. My work covered the primordial sources and modern-day manifestations of conflict between the Arab states and Israel. I addressed where the sources of conflict began, how they evolved, where they are to date, and offered a prognosis. It was a significant research project—mostly to me. It helped me bridge and reconcile the Hebrew and Arab in me, the Jewish, Christian, and Muslim, and further understand my quest to bring these circles together.

Upon my return to London, the student government at LSE brought up a motion to have the university divest from Israel. The Boycott, Divestment, and Sanctions movement (or BDS) had been gaining popularity across campuses worldwide, and I had very mixed emotions on the issue. While I empathized with the plight of Palestinian people throughout much of twentieth-century history, I also fully understood the need for a Jewish state, given my grandparents' experiences during the Holocaust. I was torn. Sara, my flatmate and friend from Queen's, offered me some advice that stuck with me forever. She said, "You don't need to divest of something in order to invest in something else." She told me that if I empathized with the Palestinian cause, I should support it and invest in it. It suddenly became clear to me that politics didn't need to be a zero-sum game. Together, we campaigned on campus to raise funds for a charity that provided medical and humanitarian relief to Palestinian children, rather than engaging in the toxic and negative BDS debates that others were having around us.

I lived in London until the following October, when I graduated with a master's degree in comparative politics and conflict studies. Then, beginning in late 2007, the financial markets around the world crashed. I'd spent all this time studying politics and economics and earning a master's degree, and suddenly it seemed as though no one was hiring, let alone a foreigner without a UK work permit. After months of searching aggressively, I could see that it was unlikely that I'd find a job in London. Grandmother did what she said she would do, but after I graduated, she wasn't going to continue paying for my ritzy lifestyle in London. Raph was a French citizen, so he found a job and stayed in London. Meanwhile, Sara returned to Canada, while I went home to Egypt.

———

In Egypt, I worked a simple gig as an underwear model while looking for acting jobs and working for Dad at his restaurants. While I was there, Natasha came to visit again. My cousins Mikey and Jessica came to Egypt for the first time, too, and I took pride in showing them around, so they could see for themselves the beautiful country I'd spoken of. I wanted them to see how much I loved Egypt, the archeological sites, and the beaches, and how wonderful the people are. I reunited with old friends from before college and became much closer to my brother Karem. I'd always felt that Egypt was a big part of me, but it was during that year that I realized I'm not *part* Egyptian—I *am* Egyptian.

I was still looking for jobs in my field of study while Dad was going through yet another divorce, making it uncomfortable to remain in Cairo. I returned to London in 2009 to continue my job search. Natasha told me that she had a spare bedroom and that I could live with her, so I accepted. It wasn't long before I discovered there were things about her that I didn't know. I was watching television late one night when I heard Natasha's voice in one of the advertisements. When I asked her about it, she told me that before working at a hedge fund she was a glamor model—doing late-night commercials. She was a pro at using her sexuality to advance her career. Living with Natasha taught me that I, too, could use my sexuality and charisma to get ahead and to possibly find that perfect job. When I thought about it, almost everyone I knew did this on some level. I didn't think it was a big deal and considered it harmless—what could possibly go wrong?

Like Natasha, Raph, and my other friends, I was finally ready to become independent, and I could do that if I found a job in the banking sector. Opportunities in London were still limited; I continued searching online, but I kept coming up short. As part of my morning routine, I went to the gym, which kept me in great shape and helped to relieve stress. But one day, an impetuous decision changed my life.

The rain was hammering down that morning when I darted through the revolving door of the luxury building where my fitness center was located. As I removed my hat, drenched, I bumped into one of two well-dressed gentlemen standing in the lobby.

"I'm sorry about that," I said politely.

"Good morning. Are you here for the job interview?" one of the men asked, suggesting I was the individual they were waiting for.

"Excuse me. The interview?" I repeated.

"Yes," the same gentleman replied, handing me a white handkerchief to dry my face. "For the chief of staff position."

I glanced down at the informal workout attire I was wearing and then back up to the gentleman. "Yes?" I told him, because I was desperate for an opportunity.

"Do we have your résumé?" he continued.

"Uh—I forgot it at home."

"Well, we're running late. This way," he said. I followed them up to an office, as the gentleman who had greeted me explained the opportunity. "You seem to be what the sheikh is looking for, but you must know that he's a fairly quirky member of the royal family and . . . rather eccentric." Out the corner of my eye, I noticed the other gentleman nodding in agreement. "Some of your job responsibilities would require you to ski and be able to live on a yacht for extended periods without suffering seasickness." I looked at him as if I'd landed in the middle of a prank. But if this really was the job description, I had literally walked into an incredible opportunity. When we reached the office, I sat down, listened, and answered their questions about my educational background, work experience, and language skills. Afterward, he told me they didn't have my name on the interview list, but that I was more than qualified.

"Are you interested?"

"It sounds like a dream job. I get to ski, live on a superyacht half the year, sail around the world, and work for a wealthy sheikh in the Gulf Cooperation Council—of course!"

At the end of the interview, he told me that our conversation was to be kept private and that I was to be discreet about the job if I was moved on to the next stage of interviews. The other gentleman, who hadn't said a word, handed me a business card, while the one speaking asked me to send my résumé and said he'd be in touch.

"You will have it this afternoon," I said.

"One more thing," he added.

"What's that?"

He pulled out his phone and snapped a picture of me.

After leaving the interview, I called my parents and told them everything. They knew I was hoping to make it to the next round of interviews because the person I'd be working for owned several large companies and was heavily involved in the global financial system. I'd be able to utilize my degrees, languages, and vast experience with international travel to cultivate relationships with ultra-high-net-worth individuals and VIPs. Mom couldn't be more excited that I'd live with a royal billionaire, travel the world privately, and spend time on a yacht. I had experienced that lifestyle with Grandfather and Grandmother, and she was happy that it could continue. However, Dad wasn't impressed; he advised me to be cautious.

"You know we've worked a lot with people from the GCC. Be careful," he said sternly. "The culture is different."

"Don't worry," I replied confidently. "I can take care of myself."

Two weeks went by, and I'd nearly forgotten about the job. I decided that the guy who was supposed to be interviewed had showed up and had gotten the position. But at the beginning of the third week, the interviewer called and told me I was moving on to the second stage.

"A private plane will be waiting to take you to the Gulf to interview with the sheikh. When you land, there will be a personal assistant who will take you to the estate."

"When?"

"This evening."

"I'll be ready."

"And, Mr. Sharif, he usually only hires British gentlemen to work in the capacity you are interviewing for. The sheikh prefers their traditional style of dress—British country clothing and tweed jackets. Wear a suit."

I told him it wasn't a problem and hung up the phone. Natasha was in the living room with me when I took the call. She heard part of the conversation and I filled her in on the rest, including the fact that I only had a few hours before catching a flight to the Gulf for an in-person interview. Excited for me, she dropped what she was working on and dove into my preparations, washing my clothes and helping me pack a small bag for the next two days while I completed a million other errands. Later that evening, I received a call that a car was downstairs to pick me up. The driver dropped me off at a private airfield near London, where I took a red-eye to an unspecified location in the Gulf to secure the job.

7

Omar of Gayrabia

The plane landed just before 5:00 a.m. in the GCC. An assistant, with jet black hair and heavy streaks of gray around his temples who was dressed in a neatly tailored dark-blue suit and a crisp white shirt, was waiting in a black SUV to transport me to the estate. He introduced himself as Hani and told me he'd worked for the sheikh for over thirty years. His hands were soft, like his voice, and his eyes were kind. Hani said, "When we arrive, we will wait outside his bedroom quarters until he wakes up. He'll want to interview you right away. Afterward, you will join him for breakfast."

"And what should I call him?" I asked courteously.

"The sheikh," he replied.

When we arrived, I noticed not just the massive estate itself, but also the sound of exotic birds and a beautifully manicured lawn that surrounded an arboretum—a perfect sanctuary from the desert heat. When I entered the palace, everything was next-level ornate, with marble, brass, and gold everywhere the eye could see—it looked as though Louis XIV had furnished the place personally.

Hani caught sight of me adjusting my blue and silver Bulgari tie. He said, "You'll get used to it. The air conditioning is on full blast, but it's always this hot—unless you're in the mountains or at the farm." Then he reached for my bags and handed them to a young man who'd come up beside him. "Don't worry about your bags. They'll be taken to your room. We're going to prepare for the sheikh to wake up so he can meet with you."

I followed Hani down a long, intricately patterned marble hallway with opulent pieces of art displayed on cream-colored pillars that were spaced evenly along the way. We sat outside the sheikh's private quarters on a decorative, velvet-tufted bench from 5:45 that morning until he rang a bell at 7:00, summoning Hani and a handful of young men. They hurried through the heavy, golden double doors and began tending to the sheikh—placing his coffee in front of him, lighting his pipe, and doing whatever else of what appeared to be a standard morning routine. I took mental notes as I watched through the doors that had been left slightly ajar. Ten minutes later, Hani returned and said, "Okay, the sheikh is ready to meet with you."

I didn't know what to expect when I entered the enormous bedroom, but the mild, sweet smell of oud and tobacco quickly greeted me. An extremely attractive young man, who seemed barely twenty, with blond hair and a lean physique, was pulling back the curtains around the room. *Good Morning America* was on the large projection screen, although it was not yet morning in the US. The sheikh lounged in a massive bed with a stack of mail beside him; I spotted my résumé lying on top of it. Using his pipe, he motioned for me to sit on the sofa alongside the bed, and then Hani seated himself next to me. The sheikh appeared to be in his mid-fifties and in rel-atively decent physical shape, with light, graying stubble shadowing his cheeks. He lowered his eyeglasses and peered over them while drawing a trail of smoke into his mouth.

"Is it true that you are Omar Sharif and Faten Hamama's grand-son?" he asked, already knowing the answer.

"Yes, it is."

"Your education is very good. The London School of Economics is impressive."

"Thank you, sir," I replied.

I found it surreal that I was being interviewed while he—the sheikh—sat in his bed. He asked several in-depth questions about my background, the languages I spoke, and my fluency in each. Then he told Hani he had to go to the bathroom. Dressed in a traditional white gallabiya with gray stripes, he swung his legs over the side of the bed and sat on the edge facing me, giving me a clear view up his nightgown. My expression didn't change, but I remember thinking, I haven't known the man for thirty minutes, and I've already acciden-tally seen his penis. He got out of bed, while Hani followed him to the bathroom. When he returned, he climbed back in bed and con-tinued the interview. After the sheikh finished asking me questions, he announced that he was going to shower and get ready. He told Hani he'd meet us in the garden room.

There were stone sculptures placed around the garden room. Wild animals romped through tropical leaves and vines on the vi-brant wallpaper, lending the room a rainforest vibe. We sat down to a delightful breakfast, prepared by the chefs, but I didn't eat much. I continued to learn more about what he needed in a personal assis-tant and chief of staff. From what I could tell, Hani seemed quite qualified, but perhaps my education appealed to the sheikh for other reasons, or perhaps Hani just needed more support.

After breakfast, the sheikh told me to change into athletic wear because we were going for a bike ride. He wanted to show me around town, as it was possible I'd soon be living there. The problem was that I'd only packed enough clothing for two days. That didn't matter; the sheikh insisted that I go with him, so Hani loaned me shorts and a pair of tennis shoes.

We went biking with one black SUV in front of us and another trailing behind. There were two guards on bikes flanking us as we casually took a path along the gulf's coast. After a few miles and some light conversation, everything was going well, and we returned to his estate.

"Okay, we're done our exercise. Put on a swimsuit; we're going into the hot tub, steam room, and cold bath. It's great for the heart."

I thought it was weird for an interview, but it had been explained that part of my job description was to be wherever the sheikh was and to do whatever he wanted. I rationalized it until it made sense. Everything was fine, and the conversation continued. I spent most of the day with him doing activities and talking in between each.

"Okay," he began, clapping his hands together. "This is going really well. But in order for you to take this job, you need to be here twenty-four seven," he said, studying my reaction.

"That's fine," I replied eagerly.

"You don't get any days off, or weekends, but you will be given a long break each year. I need to know that we really get along and that you fit into the culture here."

"I'm sure that won't be a problem."

"I'm sure. But as part of the interview process, I'd like you to extend your trip for a week."

"I appreciate that, sir, but I only packed for two days. I don't have what I need to stay longer—"

"You will have everything you need."

Hani reached into his pocket and handed me a wad of money, and that afternoon, he took me shopping for clothing so I could extend my trip.

The following week, Hani provided a daily itinerary and left me to work more closely with the sheikh each morning. Hani intermittently returned, assessed my progress, and offered general direction. Afternoons were reserved for visits to some of the sheikh's businesses and for shopping—where he'd spend thousands of dollars on a single trip. Afterward, he'd take out one of his extravagant cars and drive it recklessly, seeming to enjoy the thrill and the inherent risks.

During that week, I observed his entire staff working and communicating like one big family. Although I never asked why there weren't any women working for him, the sheikh casually explained he liked to be around other men because he didn't have any remaining immediate family. His parents, four brothers, and sister were deceased, leading me to believe that he considered those living and working with him his new family.

Three international chefs on staff prepared the sheikh's favorite cuisines so he could eat whatever he wanted, whenever he wanted it. His employees and staff dined at the table with him, even when his friends came to visit. He had a handful of young assistants, but I never knew what their exact job descriptions were. They seemed to be, well, just *there*, and Sami, a nineteen-year-old, golden-blond, handsome Lebanese man with a tapered beard, was one of them. Other than Hani, Sami seemed to be the closest to the sheikh.

Not only was Hani well-versed on the sheikh's schedule and routine, he also helped me quickly become acclimated to the staff, the city, and the sheikh's corporate team. By the end of the week, I was comfortable within the position, and it was exactly what the recruiter had promised.

I returned to London, packed up the rest of my belongings, and moved to the Gulf. The sheikh was eccentric, but also welcoming, lonely, and kind. My official title was chief of staff, which made me feel that I was a valuable employee and that he would lean on me professionally. It appeared to be a dream job. Each morning, Hani and I alternated reading a hundred or so emails and organized them by importance. Then the sheikh would go through them. I made sure the cars were ready and the plane was prepared when he traveled. I went to the office with him, arranged his itinerary, scheduled meetings with consultants or lawyers, and attended each of them to take notes. I worked directly with his professional team, which allowed me to learn more about the global financial system and the banking industry in a practical manner, rather than the theoretical way my studies had offered. More importantly, I had a brilliant, powerful, and successful mentor. The sheikh was dealing with other royalty, heads of state, and CEOs around the world. I was his right hand and quickly became a sounding board. With his connections and relationships—and with that type of power—the sky was the limit.

The sheikh had a private plane and often seemed eager to take off somewhere. One week, a visiting friend of his recommended that we go to Beirut, as the sheikh had a home there. The friend thought it might be good for the sheikh, since he'd been narrowly focused on business during the economic downturn. The businesses had required all his attention to turn them around amid the global recession. The staff was happy to prepare for the trip, as many of them were Lebanese. It would be my first time traveling to Beirut, and frankly, after a few weeks in the Gulf, I was ready to go, too. The desert, dust, heat, and humidity became monotonous for everyone. I welcomed the change, and the staff told me Beirut promised good times and good food.

Despite the recent warfare—bullet holes in buildings and bomb markings on the walls—there was so much wonderful energy in Beirut. I could feel the positivity and love for life from people wherever we went. They had the most vivacious spirit. I could still see evidence of why Beirut had once been called the Paris of the Middle East, and why my grandfather always spoke so highly of his time there while on break from filming *Lawrence of Arabia*.

At the sheikh's luxurious Beirut property, we kept the same routine, except that in the early afternoon we'd take Hummers into the mountains, going from a temperate climate to snow in a half hour. One afternoon, we were caught in a snowstorm; it was difficult to see anything, even the end of the road. At one point we hit a snowbank, which fortunately stopped us from plunging off a cliff. Other vehicles had to come and retrieve us. But even with that event, the trip seemed to put the sheikh in a better mood. When we returned to his home that evening, he said, "I'm so happy we came here; my libido is starting to come back."

Our time in Beirut marked my first month working for the sheikh and everything had gone well, especially with his businesses. It appeared that he was beginning to feel more confident in my professional abilities, but I wasn't necessarily comfortable with all of his personal relationships. Some of the men who came to visit during the week in Beirut were different than I'd seen in the Gulf. They brought with them young men who they would then touch and grab at inappropriately. They were treated as property and forcefully handed one drink after another. Because the sheikh surrounded himself with men, I had begun to suspect that the sheikh was gay. He'd once asked me if I was gay, and I'd told him the truth. I didn't want to lie, because I wanted the job and suspected he may have known anyway, but he never admitted to anything. He just nodded, acceptingly. I was happy to feel accepted and appreciated.

The fourth night in Beirut, I had excused myself after dinner and gone to my room. The sheikh had a large, festive gathering of friends, and I was sure he wouldn't miss me with the collection of young men that were present. But he knocked on my bedroom door a few hours later.

"Omar, Hani is asleep. There is a young man outside. Can you give him this watch?" he asked, handing me a small box. "And this," he added, passing me a stack of money.

It was my job to pay some of the bills. I walked outside and saw the young man standing there with his head down. I didn't know how young he was, but he didn't look of age, and that made me extremely uncomfortable, so I turned around and went back inside.

I walked past one of the assistants and said, "This is wrong," and continued down the hall to Hani's room. I knocked on his door, and he eventually answered.

"I don't know exactly what this is," I said, shoving the box and the money into his hand. "I will do anything I'm asked to do professionally—but I will not play a part in paying that boy."

"Just go and give him the money and the watch. It's fine," Hani insisted, rubbing his eyes.

"No. I will not."

"Don't worry, Omar. It's normal here," he said with disinterest, confirming my suspicions.

"Good," I replied, "You're from here, so you can pay him. I won't be involved in this," I added before walking away.

As I was heading back to my suite, one of the butlers who had overheard the exchange stopped me and said, "Omar, no one says *no* to what the sheikh asks or . . . they won't be here anymore."

"So, he can fire me. I won't be a part of that," I said.

"No, Omar. Not fired." He leaned in and whispered, "Worse."

He had no reason to lie to me. I returned to my bedroom, locked the door, and sat on the bed, wondering what I'd gotten myself into. My legs started trembling and I felt sick. I didn't know what to do.

A few days later, we returned to the Gulf, and things were beginning to change. For the next few weeks, the sheikh wasn't as communicative with me as he'd been. Sami was going to his room at odd hours, spending more and more time with the sheikh. I began to worry that I was going to be out of a job because the sheikh didn't require my services as often as he had initially. But it was beyond my control, and after the warning, I didn't know if working there was even worth it.

Soon, the kindness the sheikh had shown ended. His polite demeanor became boorish; he'd sometimes walk past me in the hall and burp in my face, without saying a word. I'd ignore him and walk away, contemplating the absurdity of his behavior, but in a short period of time, the conversations in the house began to shift. The sheikh wasn't speaking to me directly. Other assistants would tell me what he wanted me to do. I heard a few more stories from his assistants and butlers about what happened to people who had said no in that house. They had car accidents, sudden unexplained illnesses, or were just never seen again. I chose not to believe them.

The next morning, I worked with the sheikh, convinced I could still turn our working relationship back around, but he didn't seem to be listening while I read his emails. He got up and interrupted me. "I'm going to go wash; come with me so you can keep reading my emails. Bring a chair with you."

He had me place the chair next to the toilet while he defecated; I sat there reading his emails, feeling totally dehumanized. And then he lit his pipe and seemed to enjoy drawing smoke in and blowing it out in my face. I justified his behavior by assuming this was just one of those weird cultural things that Dad had warned me about. They're different—*they're tribal*—was what Dad had said.

The sheikh owned a farm in the Gulf that he'd only take a few people to; compared to the estate, it was small. He asked Sami, a chef, a butler, a security guard, and me to go along on a visit. This time, he didn't take Hani. The sheikh said, "Omar, you are going to ride with me." We took a red Corvette from which the speed regulating chip had been removed. He drove it so fast I thought that if he hit so much as a small rock, the car would flip over and explode. The man was so rich and powerful that he appeared to fear nothing, not even death. I thought about the warnings I kept hearing. When people said no, they had accidents; they disappeared. I had the fear of God in me, and yet I couldn't speak up. I just clenched the seat with my butt cheeks, trying to hold on so tightly that it actually hurt when we finally stopped. I didn't know what kind of sick game he was playing or what message he was sending, but I understood it was meant to intimidate me. I knew that I would avoid riding with him again, whenever possible.

Nearly three months had passed since I started working in the Gulf. Just as the sheikh forewarned, I hadn't received a day off, but I found other ways to maintain a bit of normalcy and peace. I became close with the staff; they were my family now, too. At night, I'd usually retire to one of their bedrooms to watch a movie, talk, make light of the way I was treated, and laugh about things that happened to them. I found out some of the others had it worse than me. But, oddly, I chose to believe everything was manageable when we swapped stories. One of the chefs, Titou, was a cross-dresser, incredibly kind, and a great belly dancer. He'd play music and teach us how to dance to it. It was the little things that drew us together.

The rustic farm was the sheikh's place of relaxation; as soon as he crossed the threshold, he vanished.

I asked Sami where the sheikh had gone. He told me, "He went to his bedroom to take a nap."

"But we just arrived," I replied.

"When he does that, it means it's going to be a very long night," he sighed. "Come on. Let's take the ATVs out and have fun while we can. You look stressed."

"I could definitely use a break," I admitted.

The air was less toxic outside, and I felt free to have fun and be myself. Sami told me that regardless of which direction we looked, the property line extended far beyond what the eye could see. "There's no escape," he joked, tossing me the key to the ATV that I was going to drive. I didn't understand why they called it a farm. There weren't any crops, the dirt fields were parched, and there was no indication of livestock. It seemed like the farm was just a hidden getaway, and Sami knew every inch of it.

Exploring the property on the ATVs made me forget about everything long enough to start enjoying my time. Sami told me to watch him do a trick he'd done a hundred times before. He took off as fast as he could, accelerating to get the height he needed off an elevated part of the land, but he must've hit something. His ATV flipped midair and launched Sami in another direction.

He hit the ground hard and began to scream. He'd broken his right leg and dislocated his shoulder. I rushed Sami to the house on my ATV, and the security guard took him to the hospital in a nearby town. When I looked at the sheikh, his eyes were furious. Sami was his beautiful golden boy—his favorite—and now he was injured.

The next few nights, it was just the chef, a butler, the security guard, and me with the sheikh. The night of Sami's accident, the mood was tense. Everyone drank a lot over dinner, but I only had a couple of drinks because of how bad things had been with the sheikh lately. After I finished my second drink, the sheikh poured me another before my glass touched the table. I didn't drink it because I was beginning to feel dizzy and was struggling to stay awake. We sat there a few minutes longer, and I remember hearing the sheikh say, "I'm going to bed."

I mumbled, "Thank goodness," because I too needed to sleep. I went to my room and was about to fall across my bed when I heard a knock on my door. I barely had enough strength to open it and found the Lebanese butler, Baqil, standing in front of me. He'd drunk a lot more than I had, but he seemed fine.

"The sheikh asked if you want to join him in his room."

"I'm not feeling well right now—but I'll check and see what he needs before I go to bed."

"You'd better go now. You don't want to keep him waiting," Baqil insisted.

I don't know how much time had passed or how long I was in the sheikh's room, but the next thing I remembered was going in and out of consciousness with the sheikh naked and on top of me. I fought to snap out of whatever haze I was under, but I couldn't. When I turned my head away from the sheikh, I saw that Baqil had undressed and was climbing into bed next to us. The sheikh instructed him to hold me in place and get me aroused. I didn't want to believe this was happening, but it was. I used my remaining strength to turn over onto my stomach just so he wouldn't see me cry. He probably thought I was offering myself to him, and then—I blacked out. I don't recall saying no or telling him to stop. I don't remember being able to speak. I couldn't say no, so I shouldn't have been able to say yes, either. I felt trapped in a body I couldn't control, and I was lost—all over again.

Unaware of how I got there, I woke up in my bed, alone, unclothed, and stripped of my dignity. I stared into the darkness, trying to figure out how something like this had happened. How long had he been doing this? And then it made sense—all of it. Sami was the person the sheikh had been sleeping with. Possibly, this was punishment because he somehow believed I was responsible for Sami's broken leg and the reason he was without his companion.

I had nowhere to go, and no one could help me. All I could think of was that self-fulfilling prophecy Mom had warned me about when I told her about Gabriel. "Don't be gay. Only problems will await you—misery, heartache, and tragedy," she'd cautioned. I needed to hear her voice, but I couldn't handle hearing what she would say. I couldn't call Mom, because I didn't want her to be right—and I didn't want her to know that she was.

More than anyone, I wanted to call my father because I needed him. But if I called him, I'd have to tell him everything, and I couldn't. If I told him I was gay and he rejected me, I couldn't take it on top of all that had happened. My father and I were close, but it was to the extent of a handshake and a kiss on both cheeks. We didn't talk about feelings, and he wouldn't know what to make of the situation I'd gotten myself into. I stared at the ceiling, becoming reacquainted with the darkness, knowing I had to go through this alone.

I remember thinking it strange that I didn't cry more that night—I had been broken. Sometimes a truly broken person can't cry. Much like a broken glass can hold no water, a broken person holds no tears. Tears are for the hopeful, and hopeful people can still dream and imagine a better world. I could not.

I got up and stumbled barefoot down the dark hallway into the kitchen and turned on a dim light above the stove. A Black Forest cake with whipped cream and maraschino cherries was resting on the counter under a glass cake stand. It looked like the chef had been striving for perfection when he had made it earlier that evening, yet it went untouched. I removed the lid, pulled a fork out of the drawer, and sat at the kitchen table, contemplating with every bite. I had just been raped, and there was nothing I could do about it. There was no one I could call for help; I was so ashamed that I'd let myself get to this point. But what could anyone do? The sheikh had diplomatic immunity, and anyways, did I really want to make international headlines in this way? Could I really stand the world learning that I was gay and a victim of sexual assault? I didn't want to become a cautionary tale or to have people see me differently.

I don't remember the taste of the cake, but I ate the entire thing. I ate until the sun began to rise. I was trying to fill a sickening pit in my stomach—but it remained hollow and empty, no matter how much I consumed.

8

Trophy Boy

Once we left the farm and returned to the Gulf, I felt like I was walking on eggshells, not knowing what I might do to make them crack. I did my best to avoid being alone with the sheikh, so he wouldn't be abusive or intentionally ill-mannered toward me. I went out of my way to prevent being punished again and quietly did my work and whatever else he'd ask me to do.

My appetite disappeared, and I stopped eating lunch and dinner altogether; instead, I'd make myself tall Bloody Marys throughout the day, rationalizing that the tomato juice and vegetables made them a healthy alternative to food. In reality, I was developing a dependency on alcohol—I self-medicated, drinking to numb myself, to help me get through each day, to forget what had happened, and, perhaps in some way, to prepare myself for what might happen next. I felt like the sheikh's property. Whatever I had thought I was there to do had ended; I no longer felt like I had landed an incredible opportunity. I was sexually assaulted, humiliated, damaged, and dehumanized, and I could see only a bleak existence for my future.

I still hadn't been given a day off. When I glanced in the bathroom mirror, fatigue kept me from recognizing the reflection. My face was thin and gaunt, and my eyes no longer held the sparkle or fire that once burned; they just stared, lifeless, floating with dark circles below them. I didn't know how to change the situation, so I pushed myself to keep going, just to get through each day. Apparently, it didn't matter to the sheikh, because he was escalating things to the next level and keeping me close to him again. Sometimes he'd make a quick jaunt in his helicopter, and it became increasingly uncomfortable when he would take only Sami and me. He made it obvious that he intended to show us off to his wealthy and powerful friends.

The sheikh hadn't touched me since the farm, but he relished in telling his friends elaborate stories and lies, sharing graphic details of things he had never actually done to me. His piercing eyes would soften when he'd fix on me with his nauseating, seductive gaze, as if I were his muse—the one who helped create the fantasies as he told them. I'd lower my head and sit quietly, trying to believe the night would soon end, but his nights were long. His friends—a mix of royal figures, heads of state, and other high-profile people—shared a barrage of distasteful jokes, as if they were imperceptible to our hearing, and then each would smile at us approvingly, appearing to savor their own disgusting thoughts. "When you want a blond, you have Sami and when you want a brunette, you have Omar," one of them teased, while the others laughed. It wasn't flattering, and it wasn't funny. I felt less like a trophy boy and more like prize pig at the county fair—dirty and marked for slaughter. At some of these events, we were instructed not to wear underwear beneath joggers, so our bulges would be discernible. At others, the hosts would parade their own staff and talent before us, like some sort of sick competition. I remember one royal figure giving me a tour of his palace, during which he pointed out a window that revealed what seemed like several hundred partially nude South Asian men, frolicking like deer on his lawn. "Those are my boyfriends," he said. "One for every day of the year."

After what had happened on the farm, I was wary of everyone. I made my own drinks, and I avoided, when I could, the sheikh and his friends when they started drinking and celebrating. I wasn't going to let what happened to me happen again, and I believed the sheikh knew that. Other than the derogatory sexual statements he tossed at me when he was around his friends, he left me alone. I wasn't sure if it was because he didn't like me, or because I didn't do the things he wanted. The reason was unimportant—I was relieved.

There were occasions when the sheikh indiscriminately decided to take a flight from one place in the Middle East to another, and sometimes he'd fly to London or New York. After breakfast one morning, he told us to pack. "Let's go to Syria," he exclaimed, as if the thought had pounced into his head randomly. That morning, he flew Sami, a couple of assistants, a few butlers, and me to the capital city, Damascus, where we stayed at the Four Seasons Hotel in connected suites. The second night there, one of his security guards woke me up around 2:00 a.m. "The sheikh says to get up and get dressed." That sickening feeling returned. I needed to vomit, but I had to pull it together. I slipped into a pair of dark jeans and a sweater before going into the sheikh's suite.

"We're going out," he announced.

I'd only gone to bed a few hours before. The sheikh didn't say where we were going—he rarely did, but I knew not to ask. As instructed, I followed him down to the lobby, where one of his security guards and an assistant were waiting. I climbed into an armored van with a gnawing feeling in my abdomen. No one said a word. The driver already knew where we were going because he took off quickly, leaving the city lights far behind us.

We drove for about forty-five minutes to the outskirts of town, an old and desolate industrial area full of what appeared to be abandoned factories. A few minutes later, the driver made a sharp turn onto a road that would have gone unnoticed to anyone who did not know it existed. When the driver parked, the sheikh said, "Just Omar and I are going in." As we got out of the van, his security guard handed me an empty black duffle bag. In a nearby warehouse, we were greeted by a young man and his father, who seemed to know the sheikh well. I kept looking at the young man as though we knew one another, but he didn't say anything, so neither did I. He reminded me of Rayan, the handsome Jordanian I'd met in Mykonos. I forced myself to think of anything else; the memories of freer and happier times were almost too much to bear in my current circumstance.

The building looked like an old slaughterhouse. When we went inside, I couldn't fathom why the sheikh had taken me to such a run-down and unsettling place. There were several pieces of farm equipment and crates sloppily stacked in scattered piles. The floorboards barely looked like they could handle the weight of the machinery. Without saying a word, the young man motioned for me to follow him. I looked at the sheikh and he nodded for me to comply. He led me to the back of the building, where he knelt down and pulled back a filthy piece of ivory and blue carpeting to reveal thick, uneven, and tattered floorboards. He put two fingers through a small notch, lifted the hatch, then turned to me, and said in Arabic, "Go down." I looked into the hole and saw the top of a ladder, but it descended into complete darkness. He repeated more firmly, "Go down!"

I looked at him and shook my head.

"They're coming. Go down," he insisted sternly in Arabic, trying to corral me into the hole and down the ladder. I didn't hear the sheikh coming, nor did I know what to expect. My mind raced. The heavy beating inside my chest made me feel like I might pass out. I tried to rationalize what was happening, but it was impossible. I didn't know if he was going to lock me down there or put a bullet in me and leave me to die, because I hadn't paid the boy, because Sami had gotten hurt, or maybe because I was no longer of any use. Maybe it was just to get rid of me, the evidence, after that night at the farm. I began to sweat and shake.

I jumped when I felt the young man's hand on my back, nudging me down into the darkness. I was terrified, and my body was taut. I was in a warehouse, in the middle of the night—in Syria. My family and friends—no one knew I was even here. I didn't know what to do, so I stepped onto the ladder, gripping it with my sweaty palms. I took deep breaths, exhaling slowly, as I lowered myself into the hole, waiting for the gunshot. I prayed that it was just my mind overdramatizing the reality. When my feet touched the uneven ground, the young man followed me into the hole and, with a few steps, reached over my head to turn on a light hanging from a ceiling covered in cobwebs. My eyes widened and my mouth fell agape. There was nowhere for me to move; I was surrounded by troves of treasure and antiquities. Apparently, the sheikh had brought me late-night, black-market antiquity shopping. The underground area resembled the storeroom of a small museum filled with numerous artifacts, some priceless. When I heard heavy footsteps, I turned around to find the sheikh carefully climbing down the ladder, the young man's father following behind.

The sheikh pointed at something and said, "Omar, wouldn't that make a lovely coffee table?"

I looked at the item he was pointing toward and saw an Egyptian sarcophagus. It was the type I'd seen in Egypt when traveling with Grandfather on the Nile.

"I don't think that would make a good coffee table," I replied. "There used to be a dead person inside of it. I don't think we should be desecrating someone's tomb."

I didn't know where it came from, but it didn't matter—the sheikh bought it anyway. He left the warehouse, delighted with his purchase, and I was just pleased to still be alive. We spent the next two days visiting his friends and traveling around Syria, which remains among the most beautiful countries I've ever visited. Especially after that scare, everything I experienced that week seemed more wonderful given the alternative.

We returned to the GCC, but I never saw the sarcophagus delivered to the sheikh's estate. I couldn't imagine it being in his living room as a coffee table. It belonged in a museum.

———

The next trip came just a few days later; we flew to New York. The sheikh had an elegant townhome on the Upper East Side, with well-known celebrity neighbors. The shopping, food, galleries, and museums attracted him to that area. He had an affection for art. His friend, a respected artist, promised to show him some extraordinary pieces while in town. Upon meeting the artist, something immediately made me extremely uncomfortable, so I made myself scarce during his visit.

Regardless of where we traveled, each day began the same as every other, and the sheikh never took a break from exercising, either. He was definitive about what he wanted to do and where he wanted to go; in New York, Central Park was one such place. He enjoyed riding his bike, but as much as he loved going out to exercise, he didn't like pedaling his bike uphill. Whenever there was an incline or slight elevation, he'd whistle, and the two bodyguards riding along each side of him moved in closer. He'd place a hand on each of their shoulders while they pulled him up the incline and then he'd go back to riding by himself. Everyone around him knew precisely what he wanted at every moment; even a simple whistle called for a specific action.

The sheikh continued his compulsive shopping in New York. We went into a record store with his security detail, and they walked down the aisles beside him with a few shopping carts while the sheikh stretched out his arms and knocked random items into the carts. When we began loading everything at the checkout, the cashier looked at us in disbelief, as if it were a joke. When we returned to his townhome, he told me that my job for the next few weeks was to upload all the CDs to his iTunes library. The tasks the sheikh assigned me no longer involved banking or gave cause for me to use any of my professional skills. He'd transitioned my role to menial labor, working to intentionally fracture my mental state and to remind me that he was the sheikh. In response, I began to drink more. In retrospect, I had totally lost my sense of self-worth—I was broken down, full of shame and misplaced guilt. I didn't leave because I actually didn't believe I deserved better.

———•———

After a week in New York, we boarded his plane and took off for his U.S. cottage in the mountains for a few weeks. The only thing I thought about was being home in Egypt and Canada. I had never imagined that I could miss my family as much as I did, even though I'd always appreciated how special it was being with them. If I had been given time off, I would have been able to keep to my work routine, just as the sheikh did, but he wasn't offering.

We were taking trips more often, and flying with the sheikh wasn't easy. The problem wasn't wearing the required suit, tie, and dress shoes but that, occasionally, the staff had to take turns using the seats and stand for part of the flight, which was uncomfortable. When the sheikh was tired, he'd have the butler fold the leather sofa into a bed, so he could put on his pajamas and sleep during long flights. The sofa happened to be the seats that we should have been seated in, so we would stand for hours on end.

The flight from New York to the mountains was somewhat choppy that morning due to rough winds, but with just five minutes to landing, the sheikh said, "Omar, go make me some tea."

"The seatbelt sign is on and we're about to land," I reminded him.

"Don't worry, I own this plane—and the pilot. You don't have to follow the rules. No one's going to yell at you but me. Go make my tea!"

As the landing gear was deployed, I unbuckled my seatbelt and hurried to the galley to make his tea so I could hand it to him before we touched down. Typically, one of the chefs or butlers served him, and a butler was on the plane. I didn't mind making it, but before then, he'd never asked me. When I reached out to hand it to him, he pointed for me to place it in the cup holder. As we touched down, I stumbled backwards, spilling the tea and burning myself—and he erupted with laughter. The sheikh hadn't wanted tea at all but had asked me to make it as a joke or to amuse himself in some perverted way. He'd wanted to see if I'd burn myself carrying it while the plane landed.

Part of the job description entailed being able to ski, and we did that the next afternoon, which was a reprieve. The fresh snow and crisp air temporarily removed some of the uneasiness I carried, providing much-needed time to recalibrate. When we returned to the cottage, the sheikh's head of security asked to speak with him. He told the sheikh that Baqil, the Lebanese assistant who had climbed into bed with us that night, had been stealing watches from the sheikh's collection and sending them back to his family in Lebanon. The sheikh gave me a dismissive glance and said sternly to his security guard, "Follow me." They went into his office just a few feet away and closed the doors.

I was in my room completing the onerous task of uploading the sheikh's CDs one at a time when I heard loud groaning from the next room. Seconds later, there was a thump. I jumped out of my chair and ran into the adjoining bedroom to find Baqil violently convulsing on the floor with foam oozing out of his mouth. The same security guard from earlier was standing over him. He pulled out his phone and dialed the paramedics while I dropped to the floor, scooped Baqil into my lap, and pulled him up against my chest. Attempting to stop his shaking, I wrapped my arms and legs around his convulsing body, but it didn't help. His teeth chattered as if he had just been pulled from a frozen lake. By the time the paramedics arrived and took Baqil away, he was still alive but unresponsive.

The next morning, I asked to visit Baqil, but I was told that the small local hospital wasn't equipped to handle his condition and that he had been taken to a larger facility nearby. Someone explained that Baqil had a pulmonary embolism in his lung and that he was being treated. I was taken aback by what happened, but no one else seemed to be; everyone who worked for the sheikh minimized the seriousness of what happened to Baqil. None of them would dare cross that invisible line and jeopardize their job or life.

The artist from New York came to visit the sheikh's lodge the following Friday. While we were having dinner, the sheikh began his graphic commentary, lying about the sexual things he did to me. Although he didn't say it, I felt as though he was selling me at auction or driving up my price for the artist. Just as I had before, I sat at the dinner table with my head down, barely picking at the food on my plate. I listened to each disgusting detail, wondering if his friend actually believed him. When I briefly made eye contact with the artist, I found him gawking at me as though he was hoping everything the sheikh described was true. This time, warning alarms went off in my mind immediately. It felt reminiscent of what had happened at the farm.

The sheikh poured vodka, one drink after another, expecting me to take it each time, and I did. But I'd get up and go to the bathroom, pour it down the drain, and refill my glass with water. I could tell the sheikh was assessing my behavior when he asked me to belly dance for them with Titou. I couldn't think of a way out. Even though Titou complied with the request, he was despondent, as if he were trapped, and I was no different. This was becoming my reality—my life. Trying to keep the evening light and fun, Titou put on some lively music and zills. We danced as instructed, but my mind was occupied with what had happened to Baqil—to Titou—and to the others before me. I couldn't erase from my mind the look of terror on Baqil's face or the feeling of how awful it was to see him in that state, especially because I still didn't know whether he had survived.

Thirty minutes later, the sheikh nodded to his friend as he got up. He came over to Titou and me and said, "I'm going to bed now." Then he leaned closer to me and said firmly, "Remember, it's part of your job description to entertain my friends, too." He left the living room and went to his bedroom. The imminent feeling that I'd been placed in a dangerous situation shot through my body. The middle-aged artist was smiling flirtatiously as he twisted the edge of his reddish-blond mustache, under the assumption that I'd drunk enough to be quite intoxicated and vulnerable to his advances—or to whatever he might soon suggest. As he positioned himself between Titou and me, I politely got up and excused myself.

Instead of going to my bedroom, where the artist might follow, I went downstairs and locked myself in the bathroom near the staff quarters. I stared at my frightened reflection in the mirror, contemplating what I'd gotten myself into. After what had happened to Baqil, I was determined to call someone in case I didn't make it out of there this time. If I didn't sleep with the artist, I believed that I would be the next to die or disappear. Sick with fear and anxiety, the only person I could think of to call was Raph. Since I couldn't tell my family, I needed someone who cared about me to know I was no longer safe. By the second ring, Raph answered, and before he could say anything, I went off on a steady rant until I got everything I needed to say out.

"I got myself into a bad situation, Raph. I'm in the United States and—and I'm going to make a run for it tonight because I don't know what tomorrow will bring."

"Slow down and start from the beginning. What situation?"

"I don't have time to go into the details. It's not safe."

"Do you need me to call anyone—or do anything?"

"No—don't do anything. This guy has diplomatic immunity. I could end up in even more trouble. I think it's best if I just disappear. They normally keep hold of my passport when I'm in the GCC, but since we're traveling I have it. I just wanted you to know if anything happens to me—I was trying to leave."

"Tell me where you are. I'll come and get you!"

"I'm in the mountains. I'll try to call you if I get out."

I hung up, leaving Raph at a loss because I hadn't told him or anyone else what was going on until then. All anyone knew was that I was the chief of staff for a wealthy businessman who inherited his fortune from his royal family and that the opportunity appeared fantastic. I was too afraid and embarrassed to tell anyone that none of it was real. I got the job because of my looks and my age. I took it because I told myself it was a real business opportunity. I stayed because I wanted to prove myself to my family, or at least not make them feel any more shame. The sheikh and I both knew the real reason he hired me and why I stayed.

I waited for what felt like a couple of hours until the cottage was completely quiet. When I thought everyone was asleep, I went up to my room and put on my boots, grabbed my heaviest coat, wallet, and passport, and left through the service entrance. Determined to make it to safety, I walked a couple of miles from his cottage down to the base of the mountain, using my phone as a flashlight. When I hit the main road, I hitchhiked my way to the nearest airport, where I bought a ticket on the first flight out that morning. When I boarded the plane, I sat in my seat, carefully constructing my resignation letter by email. But when I finished, I didn't press send. Fear was filling my chest, and it must have been plain on my face, because the woman next to me to ask if I was okay. I feigned a smile and nodded my head before turning to stare blindly out the window. Compared to all that time spent on the sheikh's private plane, this budget commercial airliner felt like complete luxury.

———•———

When the plane landed in New York City, I rented a car and headed home to Canada. I called Raph while I was driving and told him I had escaped and that I was safe, although I didn't tell him everything. He knew something terrible had happened, and that I didn't sound the same as I had before I'd left, but that was all. I spent hours brooding over the way I'd explain my random return home to Mom and the rest of my family. I didn't know what to tell them, and I didn't want to put them in danger or involve Dad or Grandfather. I definitely wanted to avoid an international fiasco. The only thing that made sense was to say I lost my job.

By now, it was late morning in the mountains, and I knew the sheikh or a member of his staff would be looking for me. I didn't want him to wake up and wonder where I was; instead, I wanted there to be an answer—closure. I pulled over to fill the gas tank, and before getting back on the road, with my hands trembling, I sent the resignation letter, in which I attempted to justify why I'd left in the middle of the night. Careful with my communication, I thanked him for the amazing opportunity, for introducing me to new people and experiences, and for showing me different places and things. I told him that I had been too embarrassed to tell him in person that I didn't think I was meant to be his chief of staff. I shared that my real passion was acting, and that I was too selfish to dedicate myself to him in the way he required. I explained that I intended to pursue acting once more and that I'd make him proud of me. Overall, my resignation was designed to defuse any tension or blame; it was meant to be thoughtful and kind, so I could leave unafraid and on good terms. In a matter of minutes, I received a reply, but I knew it was Hani because the sheikh rarely messaged anyone himself; he had us do it. Uncertain of his reaction, I pulled over to the side of the road to read the reply. It said, "Omar, good for you. If you want to be an actor, I recommend you go to acting school and take it seriously." Just reading his words made me cringe. This man was so powerful, raised like a god, that I truly believed he did not know the pain and hurt he caused. It was merely beyond his comprehension to think of the impact he had on others.

When I arrived home, I stuck to a narrative that would end all questions, and it worked. I told Mom that the lifestyle was too fast and dangerous for me, and that I was afraid. I didn't tell anyone the truth about being raped. I didn't tell them that another assistant had gotten into a car accident and died on one of the sheikh's properties. If I had mentioned Baqil, I would have broken down and confessed everything, and I refused to worry them. I felt my time there had come to an end, and if I hadn't left that night, I might not have had another opportunity to escape.

After the mountains, we were scheduled to spend all summer on the sheikh's superyacht. I was afraid that things could become worse while we were in the middle of the Mediterranean and knew that my backstroke might not be strong enough to get me to shore. On land, as long as there was a door, I could walk through it—and finally, I had.

I had made a lot of foolish choices that were dangerous and risky, but I came to understand that I made them because I didn't respect myself. Sure, the sheikh lacked empathy, but so did I—for myself. And moving forward, every decision I made needed to come from a place of self-respect. Until that point, I had been insecure; therefore, I had put myself in situations that were not secure.

9

Rock the Casbah

I'd done everything my family wanted. I'd gone to school, obtained my degrees, and had enough money to fall back on. I did everything they ever asked of me, always afraid of not making them proud, and in return, I had been wronged and raped and had repeatedly feared for my life. But here's the thing about being dehumanized—being reduced to nothing, feeling hopeless and helpless—I lost my fear. That's the difference between desperate and destitute; to have nothing left means you have nothing left to lose. I mean, what's left to fear when you've already experienced the worst, when your soul is already crushed and buried? There's no place to go but up—things can only get better. "Put your losses in the past; tomorrow you win," Grandfather always said.

I stayed in Montreal until I made the decision to follow the sheikh's advice and apply to an acting school in Los Angeles. I went online, sent in the application, and in November, the Lee Strasberg Theatre & Film Institute notified me that I'd been accepted for the next semester. Neither my father, Grandmother, nor Grandfather would be receptive to my choice, but I no longer cared. I needed to do something that resonated with me. But because classes began in January, I let Mom know. I never disclosed what really happened in the GCC, but I believed she sensed that I'd changed because, well, I was different, quiet and withdrawn. Mom wanted to be support-ive and told me to be happy. She and my aunt Evelyn even offered to pay my rent and expenses for six months so I could focus on acting.

Along with my Egyptian and Canadian passports, I neatly tucked all the money I had inside an ankle safe, packed up my new Mercedes-Benz, picked up Gill, and headed to Los Angeles. Gill made the road trip far more exciting than it would have been had I done it alone. Our conversations and occasional stops for sight-seeing and fun kept me from thinking incessantly about what had happened. With that journey behind me, I could focus on the road ahead. We stopped in Pittsburgh for the night and went to the Andy Warhol Museum, had dinner in Kentucky, and spent a mem-orable 2011 New Year's Eve listening to live music in Nashville, Tennessee. On the fifth day, we reached St. Louis, the gateway to the West and to my future happiness, and I dropped Gill off at the airport. She flew home to begin law school, and I continued my journey west—to fulfill my American Dream. I don't think Gill had any idea of how much our time together meant, but I needed her—more than she could have imagined.

Somewhere along the way, I called Dad to give him my new phone number and told him where I was headed; Grandfather Omar was with him. When Grandfather heard that I was moving to Los Angeles to become an actor, he made his stance clear: "I gave you my name, I gave you my looks. I'm not going to give you anything else. You have to do it entirely on your own." After what I'd been through, I had to believe that I could, or that I would die trying.

What happened in the GCC altered the direction of my life; I was hungry for something meaningful, and the only thing I wanted to focus on was acting. In Egypt, I was already known by some, referred to as Egypt's favorite son by others; but in LA, I was starting over. I immersed myself in my studies and began making connections in acting class the same way I'd met people in London. In a fortuitous turn of events, I met Bruce Vilanch, Roland Emmerich, and Kevin Huvane at the Abbey, a popular gay bar in West Hollywood. Bruce told me that he had the same agent as Grandfather, whom he'd jokingly called "Cairo Fred," because Omar was as common a name in Cairo as Fred was in the United States. Our banter that night was memorable, as expected, considering that Bruce Vilanch has been writing comedic banter for the greatest stars and events since the 80s.

Bruce invited me to a charity fundraiser the next evening for the American Foundation for Equal Rights to end Proposition 8 in California. It was held at a private home in the Hollywood Hills, where Elton John would be performing. Not only did Bruce invite me, but at the fundraiser he introduced me to Bruce Cohen, who'd won an Oscar for *American Beauty*, had produced the movie *Milk*, based on the life of LGBTQ icon Harvey Milk, and was producing the Oscars ceremony later that year. While I was standing next to the two Bruces, one turned to the other and suggested, "Wouldn't it be great if this year, instead of having just female trophy presenters, we had a guy?"

Cohen replied, "Yes. How about Omar?" Those three words set things in motion.

I went to a casting, met with people from the Academy, and was selected as a presenter. Within a couple of months of moving to LA, without calling any of Grandfather's contacts or friends, I'd made unbelievable connections. Grandfather's big rise in Hollywood came with an extended entrance, filmed in one continuous shot, of him riding in from the desert on a camel in *Lawrence of Arabia*. Here I was, making my entry rapidly—on one of the biggest and most watched stages in the world. I went home that night incredibly excited. This time, being a trophy boy felt like a positive!

On January 25, 2011, I flew to Atlanta to see Magda, Grandfather Omar's only sister. My eagerness to share the news with her about the Academy Awards was interrupted the second we sat down together. Magda picked up the remote and turned up the television. A revolution had broken out in Egypt. Activists were protesting government corruption, unemployment, poverty, and three decades of power under President Hosni Mubarak's reign. On what was called the "day of rage," thousands of Egyptians marched in Cairo, as other protests took place across the country. The government cut the phone lines, cell service, and network access, including Facebook and Twitter, because they didn't want people organizing in the streets. I couldn't reach Dad, Karem, or any of our family. CNN showed scenes of tanks moving into the city, water cannons spraying demonstrators, and tear gas used to repel my fellow Egyptian citizens. Droves of people were rioting, and gunshots echoed in the background—it was terrifying. Neither of us slept that night.

I was grateful when my brother Karem called the next day to tell us that because the president's children had homes where my family lived, the tanks were moving in to protect our compound. While that should have provided some sense of relief, it only added to my apprehension. The threat was real, and I didn't know what sort of revolution this was going to be—political or economic. For now, it seemed to be just chaos. No one could have known what this thing was or how far it would go. Even if there had been a stated purpose, it could quickly transform into something else.

On the one hand, while I didn't love the fact that Egypt was an authoritarian regime under Hosni Mubarak, I did appreciate the stability and security it had provided and that there was continuous economic growth, including a slowly growing middle class. But on the other hand, the rate of progress was far too slow, and many people were excluded. I was hopeful to see people reclaim their voice and express their rightful desire for self-determination. I was torn—happy that people were demanding change, but scared because I didn't know the outcome that change would yield. There was no way of knowing how many Muslim Brotherhood supporters or extremists were hiding in the shadows. For years, Islamists had been cutting their beards and keeping a low profile so they could go out into the streets. Otherwise, they would have been arrested, jailed, or worse under the military regime.

A few days later, I returned to Los Angeles to rehearse for the Oscars while the revolutionaries continued to hold court in Tahrir Square. Since I would be the Oscars' first trophy boy, there was inevitably press around it; I saw it as an opportunity to stand up for Egypt. When the opportunity came, I spoke up and shared what a critical moment it was for Egypt—and that people shouldn't be afraid to visit Egypt, because I didn't want our vital tourism economy to collapse. I told reporters that people were finding their voice at what could be the pinnacle of Egyptian modern history. I had the platform to speak out, and I wanted people to see the wonderful Egypt that I saw—the Egypt of my grandparents. Although the period around the Oscars should have been the most exciting of my life, it was the time that I felt most afraid. I had been ready to die as a teenager and thought I might be killed in Syria, but the thought of losing the family that I loved and the Egypt that I knew petrified me most.

One day during rehearsal for the Oscars, I was waiting in the wings to direct stage entrances for talent and presenters. A notable actor and producer walked up behind me, introduced himself, and then stood directly in front of me, waiting for his cue to go on stage. As he stood there, I began to feel the back of his hand rub against my genitals. I assumed it was by accident, because of the tight spacing in the wings, but as soon as I turned slightly, he grabbed my buttocks. Memories from the GCC and the farm flooded back. Shock and paralysis set in; I couldn't move. The actor started to make small talk while he continued to touch me. Trying to be nice and defuse the situation, I told him I was Omar Sharif's grandson and also an Egyptian actor, and that I was a big fan. He replied, "If you come home with me, you'll find it easier to work in this town."

I nodded, walked away, crossed back of house, and told the stage manager, "Tomorrow, in this sequence, when the presenter comes on stage left, I'd like to be waiting in the wings stage right. I don't want to be back there in the darkness with him," I said, looking directly at the actor who had taken the stage to rehearse. The stage manager didn't seem surprised.

The day of the Oscars, my stomach was in knots as I prepared for the show. Just as I finished changing into my tuxedo, Melissa Leo, nominated for *The Fighter*, walked into my dressing room wearing an attention-catching, short-sleeved ivory lace gown with a high collar and a fabulous pair of heels.

"Is Omar Sharif here?" she asked.

"You're looking at him," I replied, adjusting my bowtie as I turned to face her. "I'm Omar's grandson, and the trophy boy tonight."

She was looking for my grandfather, of course, as OMAR SHARIF was on the dressing-room door. She'd never met him, but she admired his work.

"Do you mind if I sit down and share your changing room?"

"Of course not." I smiled and told her confidently, "You're going to win tonight."

"Do you know that as a fact?" Melissa asked.

The envelopes were sealed, so I couldn't have known, and I replied, "No, but if I were the Academy, the decision would be unanimous." Melissa began removing her heels to put on a pair of ballet slippers and I interjected, "Don't put your flats on—you're going to win—and you'll want to go onstage in your heels." Melissa smiled and kept her heels on.

I was thrilled to find out in a last-minute reveal that Kirk Douglas was going to be a presenter at the show. Backstage, he took me aside and confided in me, "Whatever's in the script, we're just going to switch it up and go big. You're not just going to walk me out there. I'm not handicapped," he joked, although he had taken years to recover after a stroke in 1996. "Whatever I do, just play along." The knots in my stomach tightened—who wants to improvise in front of a billion people watching live? That said, I knew this would be my opportunity to shine on stage for the first time. Kirk crushed it! He was the highlight of the show. He kept the nominees on their toes, stretching the reveals, and then engaged in a fake fight scene with me over his cane. We had the audience in hysterics—all unscripted. At one point, I turned to the audience and caught Nicole Kidman pointing at me and mouthing to her husband, "Who is that?" I wanted to yell, "Hi Nicole, I'm Omar!" but I restrained myself and completed our bit.

After Kirk Douglas finally opened the gold envelope and announced Melissa Leo's name, she ran on stage, gracefully bowed to Kirk, and accepted the award. Then she turned to me and yelled, "Omar!" into the microphone. I went from being an unknown in Hollywood to doing a comedic sketch with Kirk Douglas, while Melissa Leo graciously included me in her acceptance speech. I felt I had made it. Dreams are made on the Oscars stage, and even without a nomination, mine was no exception.

A lot of press was written about that night, which helped me acquire an agent and a manager in the days that followed. People were asking who I was, and I'd suddenly become a recognizable face in America—at least for fifteen minutes. I was determined to capitalize on that time. The media tracked me down for interviews, TMZ waited for me outside restaurants and movie theaters, and I was able to use those opportunities to talk further about Egypt, our nascent revolution, and my love for our people.

———

I didn't take what was going on in Egypt lightly. In February, Hosni Mubarak was removed from power after thirty years of ruling Egypt. While Egyptians were having conversations about a constitution, who belonged in a new country, and what a new country could look like, I wanted to make sure everyone had a place in it. I met Paul Colichman, the CEO of Here Media and owner of *The Advocate*. Paul invited me to lunch and told me that I had an historic opportunity to come out back home. There wasn't a voice for people living in the shadows in the Middle East, and he thought I could do a lot of good. I was concerned about the possible repercussions in Egypt. I'd seen the coverage of Cairo 52, where fifty-two men were arrested and charged with habitual debauchery and obscene behavior on the Queen Boat, a floating gay nightclub on the Nile. They were vilified by the Egyptian media, who printed the real names and addresses of the fifty-two and branded them as agents against the state. Twenty-one of the men were ultimately convicted. I saw what happened to gay people—how they were rounded up, accused, tortured, and publicly tried. I was keen to seize the moment, but I knew if I were to come out, I'd have to do it in a diplomatic, hopeful, and optimistic way.

At the time, my agents and manager advised me not to come out. They accurately surmised that I wouldn't get as many opportunities to work in Hollywood. I was forewarned that Hollywood wanted me to be exactly like my grandfather. They wanted me to have darker hair, with a mustache or a beard, and to be a suave, charismatic leading man. But on the inside, that wasn't me. I was still unsure of who I was, but I surely knew I was still broken, still vulnerable, and still not in a position of strength.

After surviving the Gulf, making it to Los Angeles, and taking the stage at the Oscars, I figured this was not only an opportunity, but also my responsibility to speak out. I thought about the legacy my grandparents had left me; it wasn't to be an actor, and it wasn't to be famous. It was what my Grandmother Faten and Grandfather Omar did throughout their lives and careers in Egypt. My grandmother had used her voice, her films, her platform, and her heart to advance causes for women. Her film *I Want a Solution* had famously helped women gain the right to file for divorce in Egypt and to emancipate themselves from their husbands. I thought about my grandfather's last five or six films—all about empathy and religious tolerance, at a time when there was so much fighting in Egypt between Muslims and Coptic Christians.

Omar, after all, was born Catholic and had converted to Islam to marry Faten. In fact, the church in Egypt had excommunicated him for this egregious act and had tried to stop his family from contacting him. Grandfather took part in a dialogue of acceptance and understanding with the films *Hassan and Marcus* and *Monsieur Ibrahim*. In nearly every interview, he used his platform to promote tolerance and acceptance. And so, I realized, my true legacy was to similarly use my platform to make a difference in other people's lives.

As I watched the unfolding situation in Egypt, I feared that a political coalition, dominated by the Muslim Brotherhood, would come to power. I saw fractured liberal groups running six or seven candidates instead of banding together. The Muslim Brotherhood supporters coalesced around one party, as we liberals lay in pieces, destined to lose the upcoming presidential election. The Muslim Brotherhood had already taken almost fifty percent of the parliamentary seats—bringing the total Islamist seats to seventy percent—and they were running a candidate for president after initially declaring that they wouldn't. I wondered what it would ultimately lead to in Egypt, and if we were about to slide backwards on a dangerous slope toward Islamic fundamentalism. Would the gains in women's rights and religious tolerance that my grandparents had fought so hard for be eradicated? What would happen to the LGBTQ community, who already suffered so much? I thought about the Holocaust and my trip to Poland. People were complacent about the Nazis during their rise to power. I was complacent in the Gulf. I'd sat back and slowly let myself become a victim. I was determined not to be silent again. I decided it wasn't just my responsibility to come out and speak up; this time it was an obligation.

I wasn't so naive to think that rights would suddenly be given to LGBTQ people in Egypt. But while we were all talking about what it means to be Egyptian, I thought it was a good time to at least be included in the conversation. The protection of minorities in a new constitution would mean not having to live in the shadows—in fear. It was hard enough to be gay and closeted in Canada; imagine fearing that friends and family might find out, while being bullied and knowing that the state too could come after you, that your very existence is illegal, and that you could be prosecuted and imprisoned—made into an example to warn other people like you. I didn't see anyone else talking about it—no voices, no faces, no Arabic public figures who were out—just some whispers in the shadows. I had to do something.

That's the funny thing about revolutions; as much as they seem structural or societal, they're actually personal. Sure, they appear to be thousands or millions of people coalescing around certain goals and desires to create change. But really, they are about a mother wanting to educate her daughters, a father wanting to feed his family, or students wanting more opportunity and economic mobility. All revolutions are made up of smaller personal revolts, with personal motivations. Revolution is personal. Collective freedom comes from individual acts of liberation. You must free yourself from the idea that you don't deserve better; only then can you unite for social or structural change. My simple act was to come out and to live free outside the shadows—free from fear, free from shame, free from bondage. The act of coming out, of loving and accepting myself inwardly and outwardly, was going to be *my* revolutionary contribution.

Ultimately, I decided that I was just going to do it. All the possible negative repercussions were outweighed by the slightest chance that I could accomplish something. After the Gulf, diminished and dehumanized, I really had nothing to lose. My grandfather had once told me not to think about the prospect of losing when gambling, that good card players focus on accumulating wins. As such, I had developed a sort of counter narrative to the common risk assessment that guides many people's decision making. Instead of focusing on inherent risk, I would consider potential rewards, focusing on hope and opportunity. Now was the moment, and if I missed that opportunity to speak, it might not come back around for a long time.

I couldn't allow LGBTQ rights to get lost among the internal divisions in Egypt. I couldn't let us forget or ignore what is often the most vulnerable, hidden, and silent segment in society, so I came out. I accepted my reality: I was born gay and half-Jewish. I wanted to belong—to be part of the new Egypt. I asked for nothing other than recognition and inclusion—no special rights or privileges—just inclusion.

My letter, published in *The Advocate*, wasn't something I wrote in a day or two—it took time, thought, and reflection. Nearly three months went by before I published it, and still I really struggled. I only had one chance to get it right. I didn't tell anyone that I was doing it, because they would have worried about the repercussions. I didn't tell Dad, because I thought it was easier to ask for forgiveness than permission. I had resolved to do it, and there was no turning back. That said, I didn't know how broad the reach of my letter would be. It was to be published in an American magazine with one of the largest circulations to LGBTQ readers in the world, and it was in the language that I spoke best. On some level, though, I thought it might just disappear or stay confined to North America. Also, I wasn't sure anyone would really care what I'd have to say politically. No one had ever cared before. But I cared, and I hoped they might, too. If I didn't say it, I would have hated myself. I wasn't in Tahrir Square. I didn't go into the streets to protest and demand change, but I also didn't give up when the liberals didn't immediately get what we wanted from our first elections. I doubled down and put myself on the line. I gave the revolution my voice, my face, and my name—and I almost gave my blood.

I was in Toronto preparing for the film *Paradise 3D*, which was set to begin shooting in the Philippines the following month, when *The Advocate* sent me a draft of the article, including a photograph I'd taken for it. I was naked and wrapped in the Egyptian flag. The image was a metaphor for the revelation of my true self, hiding nothing, vulnerable and open—and a demonstration of my patriotism.

That night, I forwarded the article to Mom because I wanted to give her a heads up that it was coming. I knew Mom would have seen it anyway—she kept a Google alert set for my name—but I still didn't presume it would reach Dad in Egypt.

In the middle of the night, Mo, an Egyptian friend of mine from Queen's University, called.

"Yo, Junior—what did you do?" Mo questioned nervously.

"What do you mean?" I didn't know the article had come out yet.

"I just got a call from my brother in Egypt. All of Egypt is aflame and talking about your letter."

"In a good way or bad way?" I asked reservedly.

"It's bad, man. It's really, really bad."

My heart sank. I opened my computer for the first time that day and saw my letter all over the Internet—*ABC News*, the *Daily Mail*, *Al Bawaba*, *PinkNews*, *Der Spiegel*, *Fugues*, everywhere. It hadn't just stayed in *The Advocate*; it was an international coming-out story. Within hours, it was trending on Yahoo and Twitter, and the swift reaction was negative and critical.

First came sheer disgust. People called me a stain on my grandfather's name. Comments flooded in from all my social media platforms. On Arabic news programs, panels of sinister looking men with beards judged, critiqued, and insulted me, calling me *haram*, and a sinner—and fanning the flames of intolerance and rejection. News outlets in Egypt went into the streets, conducting interviews with the public and asking what they thought about me. Expressions of revulsion and hate were common. What followed was intimidation, death threats, and messages like, "If you come back to Egypt, it will only be long enough to dig you a hole."

And then came the others, the ones I would have expected to

support me, the Egyptians I knew. They were the most hurtful. They said, "He isn't really Egyptian. He doesn't have the right to talk," even though I'd spent half my life in Egypt and loved the country with my full heart. Others insisted, "He did this for attention. He just wants to advance his acting career," even though being gay has never helped anyone's acting career. No one comes out hoping to book more roles; quite the opposite. And lastly, the queer and activist communities, who said, "He's just privileged, what could he know about struggle or sacrifice?" None of them knew my story—how could they?—but it crushed me to the core, and once again, I felt totally alone. Instead of inclusion, I had achieved ultimate exclusion.

I climbed out of bed and threw on a shirt and pair of jogging pants. The messages had imparted a degree of hatred I'd never experienced before. I was depressed and at a loss about how to handle it. I never imagined this kind reaction. I'd thought my letter was optimistic and hopeful, and that it would be received as such.

Then the phone rang. It was Dad. I hadn't known it, but a few years prior, a cousin in Egypt had told Dad I was gay, but he'd never mentioned it. Dad treated and loved me just the same. My letter didn't change his mind, but it did make him worry about my safety.

"Hey," I said, hiding my concern.

"What did you do? It's a disaster here! You can never come back to Egypt! You know you can never come home!" Dad yelled into the phone.

"No, I'll come back. I can come back," I said, in flat-out denial.

The phone wouldn't stop beeping. Calls were coming in one after another.

"No, you can't! It would be too dangerous. You've given up everything. Even the right to inherit. Only Muslims can inherit from other Muslims, and you told everyone you're half-Jewish. You've given up everything!"

My father told me that Grandmother Faten was extremely upset with me, not because I was gay, but because she'd always lived her life so privately. She felt that I had put the family and myself at risk. During a time of great upheaval, I'd cast a spotlight—one that I'd avoided for so long—on all of us. I hadn't made myself a target; I'd made my entire family a target. No one knew if they were going to come after us—no one even knew who *they* were—but I'd given them a reason to. After deliberating and writing for three months, I hadn't taken any of that into consideration. My father wasn't upset with me because I was gay. He never condemned or shamed me. He was upset because he was afraid for my life, and the lives of my family members. I told him I had to go, but he continued ranting about my safety.

"Dad, I'll call you later. I have to take this call."

It was my friend Chad, a Canadian political consultant and operative, and he'd been following the news that day. He asked me to get in touch with the Royal Canadian Mounted Police, believing that I would need round-the-clock security, at least until the dust settled and things could be evaluated more clearly. I'll never forget his parting words: "Godspeed." It brought tears to my eyes and a lump to my throat.

The phone rang again; this time it was Mom, finally awake. I knew she had been watching the same coverage and reading the same messages as me, every last one of them. I didn't know what she would say, but I felt it would be similar to when I told her I was gay. The last thing I wanted to do was disappoint my mother—again. I stared out the window at the cold, gusting snow and answered.

"What did you do? What did you do?" she cried, over and over again. She couldn't say anything else, trapped again in the anxiety she'd had when I was growing up. As I slowly stepped out onto the twelfth-story balcony, my mother's crying voice became increasingly muted with every "What did you do? What did you do?" I could hear her pain, her tears, and her panic.

The magnitude of what I'd done hit me, and for an instant, the fear, pain, and thoughts of letting go returned with the same intensity I'd felt as a kid. Petrified, I stood in the blistering cold, shivering and barefoot, wondering if I'd gone too far this time—if I had finally crossed a line I couldn't come back from. Maybe I shouldn't have done it; maybe the world still wasn't ready for me. I gripped the snow-covered rail and stared over the edge, as I had many times before when I'd contemplated jumping, but this time was different. I'd finally done what I needed to do, the way I wanted to do it. I wasn't reacting to the hurt and pain imparted toward me; I was in control this time. I always thought that acceptance from others was important, but self-acceptance is paramount. I no longer needed anyone's acceptance but my own. I was out, and I was free. The burden of being afraid of what other people would say, feel, and think about me was over. The years of secrets and shame and hiding were behind me. And at that very moment, as if by providence, the snow tapered off and a beam of sun shone through the clouds, lighting up my face. I released the rail, turned around, and walked back inside, closing the patio door behind me as Mom's voice returned. "What did you do?"

"I set myself free," I confessed, and I hung up the phone.

For once I had no secrets. If there were repercussions, I'd deal with them. I didn't know what the threats of violence might bring or when they would come, but I knew that whatever they were, I would get through it.

10

A Tale of Two Omars

I was back in Los Angeles, sitting at my kitchen counter and flipping idly through my collection of magazine articles and family photographs. The beautiful photos roused emotions and memories I'd long forgotten, but they offered only a glimpse into the lives and legacies left by my grandparents. Behind their smiles and numerous accomplishments were their struggles and substantial contributions to social change. I ran my fingertips delicately across a black and white photograph of Grandfather Omar sitting comfortably in a chair. He was wearing a dark-colored sweater and had a white chapeau with black trim tilted rakishly on his head of thick gray hair—stylish as always. I smiled, overcome with a fusion of joy and sadness as I thought of the many ways we had lived parallel lives. Grandfather may never have recognized the tremendous influence he had on me, but the reflection in the mirror didn't lie; he was always there. Perhaps lending my voice to social causes the way Grandfather had done throughout

his life had been my destiny all along. Had I continued waiting for
that right moment to come out, I might never have discovered my
platform. When I took the opportunity to speak up, it changed my
life. I picked up the photo and recalled the time Grandfather was interviewed about his reason for making the film *Monsieur Ibrahim*, for
which he won a César Award for best actor. "In these times," Grandfather stated, "when we're living with conflicts all over the place, I
thought it would be nice to make a small picture with tolerance in it
and to say that we can live together and love each other, no matter
what race or religion we are." Grandfather Omar always believed that
there was commonality to our common humanity, and he practiced
and preached those ideals every day. Even as a teenager, I can recall
him counseling me before a night out with friends, "There are only
two things one must never ask a woman before kissing her: her age or
her religion." It's proved sage advice, and I've since applied it to men.
He had to learn this lesson the hard way.

———

In June of 1967, the Arab–Israeli Six-Day War broke out. At the
time, Grandfather was filming *Funny Girl* with Barbra Streisand,
with whom he was having an affair. When a publicity shot of the two
of them kissing was released around the world, it engendered much
controversy; many people in the Middle East were offended, if not
outraged. There was no tolerance, not even for a little kiss. Investors
in the production of *Funny Girl* were Jewish, Barbra was Jewish, and
the environment in Hollywood was decidedly pro-Israel. Several of
the film's investors wanted Grandfather removed and the role recast,
while others wanted Omar to issue a statement condemning Egypt.

Ultimately, the director, William Wyler, who was also Jewish, spoke out against removing Grandfather, and they kept him in the film. In Egypt, the press launched a campaign to have Grandfather's citizenship revoked, and President Gamal Abdel Nasser's regime accused him of being a Zionist spy. Grandfather wasn't afraid of being exiled or disliked, because he knew he hadn't done anything wrong. Instead, he went home, moved his family out of Egypt, and didn't return for a couple of decades. During that time in exile, he loved Egypt just the same. Omar Sharif was never a spy and simply displayed acceptance—an advocate for tolerance above all else. People just weren't ready to accede to his vision. When Grandfather finally returned to Egypt at the invitation of President Anwar Sadat—who famously made peace with Israel, earning him the Nobel Peace Prize and his assassination—it was as though he never left. He continued to love Egypt and the Egyptian people more than anything in his life—maybe even more than his family. In fact, Omar Sharif was an avid supporter of the 2011 revolution, and he called for the resignation of Hosni Mubarak, saying, "Given that the entire Egyptian people don't want him, and he's been in power for thirty years, that's enough." My grandfather stood for what he believed was right, even when it cost him. By setting myself free, I had finally done the same, and I, too, had been misunderstood. Like with grandfather, people just weren't ready to accede to my vision.

Coming out in Egypt ignited a firestorm against me. As had happened with Grandfather, court cases were launched to revoke my citizenship and ban me from my country. I'd follow the Arabic articles that documented the government and media's campaign against me, my heart tearing apart a little more with each incoming Google alert. But deep down, like grandfather, I knew I did nothing wrong.

In the midst of that storm, the global LGBTQ community and many influential people around the world showered me with messages of support and praise. I received a phone call inviting me to meet with Israeli president Shimon Peres at a state dinner hosted by the prime minister and the governor general of Canada. At the dinner, Shimon reminded me that because I was part-Jewish, I always had a home in Israel if I needed it. I thanked him for that sentiment and assured him that I always had a home in Canada, too. I also told him about my visit to Israel and joked that from the moment I landed at Ben Gurion Airport, I was given white-glove service—it was a latex glove, but I was still appreciative. He laughed awkwardly. I was even approached by a member of the U.S. Foreign Service and told that the Department of State had been following my story in Washington. Hillary Clinton had ordered all embassies to report on the state of LGBTQ affairs in their host countries, and my case had been elevated in the event that I might require or request any assistance. Despite all negative emotions I felt because of Egypt's response to my coming out, it was amazing to feel so much support from a global community.

In the weeks and months that followed, I was surprised to receive hundreds of messages, and then thousands, from LGBTQ youth across the Middle East and North Africa, who expressed appreciation that they now had someone they could identify with—they thanked me for having the courage to step out from the shadows and for giving the LGBTQ community in Egypt a face and a voice. I had no idea how impactful my story had been or how many people I had encouraged not to jump until I read those messages. They continued to pour in by the thousands and are what keep me going to this day.

I don't agree with everything the Egyptian government did to me, but if standing up to them helped a single person feel less alone, then it was all worth it. During my youth, I didn't have a face to relate to or anyone to talk to about being gay. I didn't know how to stand up for myself, because I was trapped in my own fear. My only escape was sitting on the sofa and watching shows like *Will & Grace* and *The Bold and the Beautiful.* Those shows gave me hope and kept me alive—they were as close as I came to seeing other gay people, to experiencing true acceptance and tolerance, and to understanding my own self-worth. I didn't have the support I needed, but I came to realize that maybe I could be—for the people in the Middle East or anyone who needed encouragement—what those shows had been for me: a lifeline, hope that it can get better, and evidence that some-one does care. Visibility and representation matter. Words and images matter. They are powerful devices that can be used to make us laugh or to make us cry; they can entice just as easily as they can incite. When I came out, I was attacked by the Arabic media but equally by the devastating reality that I was misrepresented to—and misun-derstood by—the masses. After living with decades of torment, and coming out to yet more criticism, I quickly realized that I had to keep pushing. My battle for acceptance had only just begun.

Following my letter in *The Advocate*, I was introduced almost immediately to GLAAD, an organization that has focused on LGBTQ visibility and representation for over thirty years. Specifi-cally, GLAAD has sought to harness the power of the media to drive acceptance and understanding, laying the groundwork for legal and legislative equality. It was the right fit at the right time, and I became their national spokesperson. The organization offered me the unique opportunity to reach large audiences quickly and in a scalable way. The news media helped share our message, my story, and the stories of others like me. It allowed us to comment and respond to breaking news, current events, and global issues. Entertainment media was just as critical in helping us accomplish our goal of worldwide acceptance, because Hollywood is the largest cultural export of the U.S. I knew that with GLAAD, I could bring about change in Egypt by challenging American media to portray increasingly progressive plotlines and characters that would increase empathy and that LGBTQ people around the world would relate to. American media could make it past Middle Eastern censors because, while people are poor in the region and may not have roofs on their homes, many have satellite dishes. Our objectives were twofold: to give LGBTQ people a reflection of themselves on television, so they could see that they were not alone, and to open hearts and minds, thereby creating more allies. The TV shows and global news outlets I appeared on garnered considerable attention in the Middle East and North Africa and helped GLAAD promote free and open societies in places once beyond its reach.

With GLAAD, I had amazing mentors, and I was fortunate to learn from leading activists. Rich Ferraro taught me about communication, message discipline, and interview techniques. Dave Montez taught me to trust my instincts and to lead with personal stories that others can relate to. Sarah Kate Ellis taught me about organizational strength and stability. Jennifer Boylan and Nick Adams opened my eyes to issues facing the transgender community, and Wilson Cruz taught me how to leverage and elevate my existing platform for good. Wilson played one of the first out characters on television, and he continues to be an inspiration for many, myself included. With this team, I have been involved in anti-bullying initiatives, transgender equality initiatives, marriage equality battles, as well as the end of the Defense of Marriage Act. On a global level, I represented GLAAD during the Sochi Olympics in 2014 when Russia introduced anti-LGBTQ legislation, which included bans on people raising the rainbow flag and holding hands in public. Russia insisted that athletes and attendees advocating for gay causes would be barred from doing so or risk arrest. Rather than accepting their threats, GLAAD put out a media handbook to help journalists keep public attention on the law throughout the games. We even reached out and met with the sponsors of the Olympics that year and convinced several of them to put pressure on the government and to go into Russia with pro-equality messages. I remember reminding several of these multinational corporations that if they claimed to have certain values in one country, those values must transcend borders. GLAAD also enlisted several celebrities to support our Olympic campaign, who used their power and influence to say and do the right thing.

While I was with GLAAD, Guido Barilla, the chairman of the Barilla Group, engendered controversy in the LGBTQ community during an interview with an Italian radio program, prompting calls for boycotts of the company. At the time, we didn't have a permanent president at GLAAD, so I welcomed Guido Barilla to our offices and sat with him. We spoke about our differences and misunderstandings, and the Barilla Group has since evolved into a progressive company that supports the LGBTQ movement worldwide. They started a diversity and inclusion board to establish goals and practical strategies for the improvement of internal policies and external engagement. I stayed involved and worked closely with their team to help identify the right people for their board, including a mentor of mine—David Mixner. As a result, Barilla implemented some of the most progressive employment benefits for the LGBTQ community, even before marriage equality became a landmark ruling.

The initial calls to boycott Barilla were helpful and lent urgency to the situation, but sitting at the table to talk and better understand one another made the most impact. By sitting together, progress can be made, lessons taught, and change implemented. Some people aren't willing to sit down together, and they don't want to change, but the power of dialogue should never be underestimated. Around that same time, I reached out to the *Duck Dynasty* cast after an interview was published that included incredibly hurtful comments about the LGBTQ community. They refused to sit down and have a conversation, and that unwillingness to have dialogue was damaging both to them and to the greater good. Freedom of speech does not necessarily correlate to freedom from consequences. It's sad when people can't see their own misconceptions or mistakes. I, for one, appreciate my mistakes; teachable moments come when you can accept that there is something left to learn. This type of education can only happen when we share our stories and understand each other on a human level.

From these experiences with GLAAD, I realized that if I was going to be successful in the activist arena, I would likely accomplish more by sharing my story, showing people who I am, and creating empathy by demonstrating all that we have in common. That became my modus operandi. If I'm honest, even with GLAAD I always felt hesitant calling myself an activist, because to me an activist is someone who actively works to change policies or laws. I think of myself, in contrast, as someone who lives his life and makes waves, leaving it up to others to decide how they'll swim in them. By the time I left GLAAD, I had found my own voice and understood my true purpose. I realized that I wanted to actively work to change the minds of people around me and to create understanding and acceptance. It was with that in mind that I sought a grant with ARCUS on the day Grandfather died. ARCUS believes that people can live in harmony with one another, and so do I. Their grant would allow me to use *my* voice, *my* way. I knew that acceptance in the Arab world would take a specific initiative—something I couldn't accomplish fully with GLAAD or more traditional activist methods. Activists wouldn't necessarily succeed where there wasn't a rule of law or constitution they could try to change. The fight in Egypt wasn't yet about equality, because equality is a legal concept. The fight was still for acceptance, which is moral and ethical. The activist methods that were being used in courts and legislatures in the United States weren't going to work back home. In the Middle East, I was up against religious interpretation and cultural attitudes.

I acquired the grant from ARCUS so that I could participate in the Oslo Freedom Forum, an event held annually by the Human Rights Foundation. The forum has become a leading platform for the voices of activists and freedom fighters worldwide and has been referred to as the "Davos for dissidents." Using personal stories of survival, strength, and sacrifice, these freedom fighters take on tyranny and oppression by appealing to hearts and minds. With that goal, I wrote a speech and traveled to Oslo. I reintroduced myself, but not as someone calling for changed laws or inclusion, as I had in my letter in *The Advocate*. Instead, I wanted to show people who I was on the inside—a son, a grandson, and someone who just wants to be loved and accepted, like everyone else. It was no longer about laws or rights; it was about acceptance and understanding. My message finally resonated.

As people began to show increased interest in my message, I was invited to continue sharing it. I became an ambassador for the Human Rights Foundation and the Elizabeth Taylor AIDS Foundation, I spoke to parliaments and legislatures around the world, I addressed the issue of LGBTQ refugees at the United Nations, and I discussed LGBTQ acceptance and called for the end of HIV stigma in front of audiences in four continents and dozens of countries. I was honored to be selected as one of several Africans who have upheld Nelson Mandela's legacy on the centennial celebration of his birth, during which I delivered a speech in Johannesburg. I was named grand marshal of several Pride Parades. Prague held one of the largest parades in Central Europe in August of 2016, and news outlets reported that over forty thousand people attended. As an LGBTQ Arab exile, the role of grand marshal of the parade, which took place in the midst of the Syrian refugee crisis in Europe, allowed me to speak on behalf of one of the most marginalized groups at the time. Many people aren't aware that Omar Sharif was of Syrian and Lebanese descent, which means that I am, too. When people think of Syria, they think of ISIS, not of families fleeing warfare or of the threats faced by LGBTQ people. Refugee is a blanket term that lumps together so many—I suppose that I, too, am a refugee of sorts, even with my means and my family name.

As a contribution, I wanted to facilitate understanding. Even when I was angry, while people were calling me names, continuing to take away my rights, and banning me from my home in Egypt, I remained calm and in control of my emotions. I always tried to maintain the higher ground, just as my grandmothers had. Faten was always poised and dignified, even when speaking about or demanding women's rights. Bubbie taught me to forgive people the moment they said something and to try and understand the root of their misunderstanding instead of taking an accusatory stance. If someone makes the choice to hate me, it is because they don't understand me. Misunderstanding is an opportunity for renewed understanding. Initially,

I deleted all the negative and hateful comments on my social media pages, but I now leave them for the world to see. Erasing hate does not eradicate it. I learned a great deal from my family, and I've tried to use it in my capacity to help others.

After everything that I'd gone through, I sought to turn hopelessness into hope, torment into testaments of strength, and to let my lesions morph into lessons. I started converting all the negatives I experienced into positives and took my message anywhere it could be heard. I traveled the world to encourage people—not to impose or to intimidate, but to be heard and to be hopeful. Those who opposed my message could disagree with me, but while I was sitting with them, we could often work through our differences and find some common ground. I was no longer trying to do the job of an activist, but rather acting as a mediator.

Even though I've been through decades of bullying, suicidal thoughts, and rape, and faced vilification by a country, exile, and more threats of violence and death than I can count, I've opted to remain optimistic. At first, I was offended when someone called me privileged, as those who did so were basing the concept of privilege entirely on supposed net worth or socioeconomic status. However, with time, experience, and accomplishments, I realized that they were right. I have been privileged—privileged to inherit the legacy of the Sharif name and privileged to inherit a platform for social change from my grandparents.

Grandfather Omar was privileged, too. He embraced and appreciated the incredibly diverse roles he was given, in such films as *Lawrence of Arabia, Funny Girl, Doctor Zhivago, Hidalgo, Che!, Monsieur Ibrahim,* and others. But he was also somewhat disappointed when he was the only person of color cast to play a Russian physician and poet, a Jew from Brooklyn, a Nazi officer, a Turkish immigrant, a Cuban revolutionary, a Spanish priest, an Austrian prince, an Armenian refugee, a Mongolian emperor, or a Yugoslav patriot. It wasn't that Grandfather didn't want a particular role or appreciate the money he made from them—Grandfather wanted to see more diversity in Hollywood. He told me that he'd ask his agent, the director, or even the producer why they didn't get a Russian actor or Mongolian and so forth, but the response was that there weren't many trained actors at the time. Casting Grandfather in Hollywood films opened the doors to discussions about casting racialized peoples in significant or leading roles. The Hollywood executives saw Omar Sharif as an actor who had the exotic look and languages to fit into the category of Other. Had they made any of his films in the present-day, they'd have had a broader range of actors to play many of his roles. By the time Grandfather reached the pinnacle of his film career, the lack of inclusion and diversity remained, but he continued to be conscious of the need for it. Grandfather was a symptom of Hollywood's problem and also a breakthrough for the end of *a* foreign person of color playing *all* other racialized peoples. There are too many barriers in acting, just as there were for Grandfather, but he used his platform to break those barriers and open doors for others. If one more person can slip through the doors that Grandfather helped to open, it's worth it—art and storytelling are privileges.

Looking at the photos and reflecting on my family history and my own reminded me of what I'd overcome and accomplished and of how much more there was still to do. Photos are just stories locked in time. In those stories are people, relationships, and lessons to impart. There is so much to learn when you look at someone's face.

When I was in Oslo, I finally told my story to the world and shared everything that had happened since I had come out. People were familiar with my letter, but they still didn't really know me. Members of the LGBTQ community are not an issue; they are not facts, figures, statistics, or moral or ethical debates. Members of the LGBTQ community are people. Through media advocacy, I'd given the movement in Egypt a face—my face. They now had pictures of my childhood, photos of me with my grandparents, and my stories of growing up in Egypt. Sharing my story and helping to elevate the stories of others continues to be the best way I know to move the hearts and minds of people before we can even think of moving legislatures. It's harder to hate someone you know.

In Oslo, after giving my address to the Freedom Forum, I was invited along with two other activists to a meeting with a high-ranking politician in the Norwegian parliament. I remember sitting in his office as the three of us discussed ways the international community could help play a role advocating for change in our home countries. After the meeting, the politician took us on a tour of the building, and at one point while guiding me into place for an official photograph, he placed his hand on my buttocks. After everything I had been through, I was still shocked; here I was at a conference to talk about human rights abuses, and a closeted politician had the audacity to grope me. I was so shocked that I didn't say anything. When we left the parliament, one of the other activists, a woman from Iran who had endured torture and imprisonment, turned to me and said, "What the hell just happened in there?" I didn't know anyone else had seen it. I replied, "Let's just get out of here." The only people I told about the incident were the organizers of the conference—so that they would never again put another person in that position. Today when I look at that photograph, it, too, tells a story.

The following day, still in Oslo, a journalist from *Süddeutsche Zeitung* in Germany asked to interview me. I agreed. After telling him my story, he asked me several questions, which I answered, and he concluded the interview by asking, "If you had one question that you wanted to ask a religious head in Egypt, what would it be?"

I replied, "Should I really be hurt or harmed for being myself?"

I thought the question was appropriate, as I was still receiving threats of violence and death. A few months after my interview, the same magazine interviewed the highest religious authority for Muslims in Egypt, the Grand Mufti. He was asked about the treatment and murder of gay people after the mass shooting in Orlando. His reply was, "It is religiously not allowed and not an accepted practice in Islam, but that doesn't give anyone the right to hurt homosexual people or to take the law into their own hands." In my view, that statement remains one of the most significant moments in Egyptian LGBTQ history. The government was still persecuting people, but for a religious leader to take away the individual ability to execute judgment or punishment increases acceptance and safety for our community—even if it is only moving the needle just a little bit. So many activists want things changed all at once, but if my story has in any way influenced the thinking of the religious head of Egyptian Muslims—that is real progress. He didn't imply that we should live freely and be celebrated or have pride parades at the pyramids and marriage equality. But it was still a significant step.

I learned to be patient and pragmatic in my approach; I learned that tiny victories are still victories. Changing a single heart or mind is a victory. If one person comes out to their family and just one member of their family accepts them, that's another victory. Even gaining allies one at a time will help the movement spread.

I didn't always heed my own advice and stay levelheaded, and there were some moments when I let my own frustration get the better of me. One example was in 2019 when the sultan of Brunei issued a law to subject LGBTQ people to stoning. In a fit of rage and haste, I tweeted that I volunteer myself second to be executed under Brunei's new anti-LGBTQ law on the condition that the sultan's son would be first, effectively outing Prince Azim, and that the sultan himself cast the first and last stones. After international backlash, the sultan backtracked on enforcing the law, but I never found any joy in the outcome or its aftermath. After long moments of introspection, I had to accept that I might have put Prince Azim's life in danger—and I deeply regret that. I could never have known or understood the prince's predicament, and it was not for me to judge his actions or lack thereof, nor to offer him as a sacrificial lamb. The tweet made international headlines, and I still feel a certain shame about it today. In fact, as I write this final chapter, I am saddened to learn of Prince Azim's untimely death at the age of thirty-eight. We were told he passed after battling a long illness, but in my heart I will always question the true cause of his death.

I am also somewhat dismayed that many people are still calling for the boycott of the Dorchester Collection hotels, which are owned by the sultan of Brunei, and publicly shaming patrons. While it is up to every individual to choose how and where they spend their disposable income, boycotts lose their effectiveness as tools when we don't end them after achieving the outcomes we demanded. I've since held

many conversations with LGBTQ employees of Dorchester Collection hotels, all of whom have expressed what welcoming environments
they have always been, while touting the company's long history of
progressive internal policies. At some point, our intention to do good
with a continued boycott of the sultan begins to hurt fellow LGBTQ
brothers and sisters, and can bring renewed harm to others.

———

When Mom finally came around and bought me my watch, it was
her way of saying she understood and accepted me—and that was
all I had ever wanted from her. It took time, but she has become
one of my most ardent supporters. She took to the initiative and
has become an advocate for LGBTQ rights. Oftentimes, those who
put up the biggest fight become our fiercest protectors. It's heart-
ening when Mom receives messages from parents whose children
have come out. Sometimes she even meets with them over a cup of
coffee or tea to encourage them to embrace acceptance. She tells
them the truth about the way she handled my coming out, admit-
ting that it wasn't easy. Her initial focus had been on what it meant
for her, which included her reputation and her future. She advises
parents not to make the same mistake of refusing to understand
their child. From her experience, Mom tells them not to be closed-
minded about what they want from or for their children. If they
are not open, they won't see their child struggling and suffering.
It was difficult for Mom to have a gay son, but she came to understand how hard it was for her son to be gay. Often, we are blind to
others and only think about ourselves, but that can change, just as
it did for my mom.

My experiences are what prepared me to better handle my life today. The bullies never went away, but what changed was my response to bullying. I was bullied in elementary and high school, in Beirut, and by the media, Egyptians, and political and religious authorities—and it hasn't stopped. But once I learned to have self-acceptance and self-love—the bullying no longer *hurt*. It was futile, weak, and desperate. People who bully others and spread hate are the weak ones.

Now that I'm acting, I embrace roles that allow me to represent my authentic self, the same way Grandfather Omar always championed. Omar Sharif didn't realize it, but that door he worked so hard to open benefited his own grandson. I've become somewhat of a go-to guy when the industry wants an LGBTQ Arab, and I've appeared on the television show *Mélange*, where I play a Syrian refugee, and in Assi Azar's hit Israeli series *The Baker and the Beauty*, where I play a gay Lebanese man in a loving marriage with an Israeli despite the characters' opposing political views. Assi was one of the first public personalities to come out in Israel and to embed his authentic self into every one of his projects. In fact, when I came out in Egypt, he sent me one of the first kind messages that I received over Twitter to say he was proud of me. When my participation in the new season of his series was announced in late 2020 it was met with large-scale criticism and backlash in the Middle East, even as more Arab states continued to normalize their relationships with Israel. Calling my decision to take the role controversial and shameful, the Arabic media keeps asking audiences, "What would Omar Sharif think if he were alive today?" I know that he would be proud of me. I can finally do what my grandparents did and use art to change people's hearts and minds. Throughout my childhood, I thought it was my job to straddle the walls between my Arab, Jewish, and gay worlds, but now I know it is my job to dismantle them. And nothing tears through walls better than art.

In February of 2019, I traveled to the Middle East for the first time since coming out. Whether in Morocco, Qatar, Jordan, Palestine, the UAE, or Saudi Arabia, I was so close to Egypt that a gentle breeze brought me the smells and sounds of my home, which I would have believed impossible. I could hear the muezzin summoning Muslims for prayer each morning and smell the burning of tobacco in the streets. When I closed my eyes, I could imagine walking along the beach with my father or sitting at Grandfather's table—having dinner with him and his friends. For moments, I even wondered what it would be like to go home and see my father, younger brother, and the family I was exiled from in 2012. When I opened my eyes, that mental picture vanished like a mirage in the desert. I still wouldn't dare let my feet cross the border—not yet. The only thing I can do is accept that I've now come closer than I've been in years and continue to hope that one day I will return.

With all I've been through, I draw on the advice from my family for strength and encouragement in difficult times. My grandparents are no longer here, but they left me with valuable life lessons and two incredible parents. Grandfather Omar inspired me to live in the present and with no regrets. When I finally came out of the shadows, I finally started to live. There is no life until you are living authentically. My letter in *The Advocate* might not have turned out the way I had planned when I wrote it, but I have no regrets. And though I might never go home to Egypt, I will always have hope.

Epilogue

Every morning I wake up to an inbox flooded with disturbing and disheartening messages out of Egypt. The messages come from friends and strangers alike, members of the Egyptian LGBTQ community I left behind nine years ago when I came out as gay and withdrew from the country, hounded by threats of violence, intimidation, and even death. The message writers are desperate to do what I did: escape a country gripped by an outbreak of homophobic persecution. Failing that, far too many of the writers say they want to escape their lives. I do not know what to tell them. I would like to offer them hope. I would like it not to be false hope.

When I came out in 2012, I wanted to use my status as a public figure to push LGBTQ acceptance through what I then worried might be our darkest hour. Unfortunately, since then conditions have only worsened, and the country is now gripped by a brutal crackdown against some of its most vulnerable citizens.

In recent years, Egyptian police have started stopping men who they suspect are gay in the streets, searching their phones for incriminating photos or hookup apps, and throwing them in prison for sentences ranging from six months to six years. There have been raids on bathhouses and on at least one purported same-sex wedding. There are stomach-churning reports that police have subjected suspects to forcible anal exams, which are—let us not mince words here—a particularly humiliating form of torture.

The supposed impetus for this crackdown was a widely circulated video from a September 2017 concert in Cairo, during which some attendees waved rainbow flags in support of the band's lead singer. The images spurred a wave of hateful rhetoric from Egyptian cultural commentators, who claimed these debauched radicals represented a slap in the face to our country's identity and goals.

These hateful messages found fertile ground in a country that is rightfully frustrated by a slow and painful pace of progress. As many frustrated societies have found, gay people make a convenient scapegoat. When we are already forced to live in the shadows, we are the perfect, faceless villains. In the photographs of the men being dragged into Egyptian jails, they all cover their faces with their shirts or their hands, hiding their shame and leaving observers to imagine that these men could be anyone—anyone except their friends or brothers or sons.

I don't talk about this with my American friends. They hear these stories with the horror you'd expect, but I can't help but think that it's laced with some faint admonishment, and behind their pity I hear: "Well, what did you expect, having the foolishness to be born gay *and* Egyptian?"

They don't know the fundamental warmth and joy I still associate with the Egyptian people, despite my exile. They don't understand the fierce patriotism and pride I feel for my country, a pride that exists for most LGBTQ Egyptians, despite their persecution. Though the country's conservative talking heads paint the Egyptian LGBTQ community as treacherous and debauched radicals, our goals are the same as the government's: security, stability, and economic prosperity. Prosperity, it bears mentioning, is harmed when Western tourists associate the country with human rights abuses and choose not to visit.

It's difficult to explain to people who came of age during the heady wave of victories for the American LGBTQ movement that our goals in Egypt are much more modest. For the most part, LGBTQ people in the Arab world just want to live in the same relative quiet that they have for generations, free from the terror that the slightest gesture or glance might betray them.

I know this fear firsthand. I was taunted in school for being different. I had men expose themselves to me in the streets of Cairo. An ex-lover threatened me with a handgun, afraid he might be outed. I was drugged, groped, assaulted, and raped by powerful men. These encounters all share a common root; I've come to understand that the closet is actually a weapon used against us. When people can hide their crimes in the shadows and when victims are too afraid to speak out for fear of rejection or reprisal, justice often goes unserved. The closet doesn't just hide gays; the closet protects the predators who prey on us.

Throughout this book, I've chosen not to name some of the higher profile predators I've encountered. That choice was not made out of cowardice, but rather out of conviction: the confidence to finally keep the focus on my story—the courage to finally be seen and heard. I've freed myself from the silence and shadows of the closet. These men have taken so much from me already; they won't get the spotlight in my story, too. My goal in writing this book was never to seek justice against those who have wronged me; though I may not have named predators in this book, that does not mean I have not pursued action along other avenues where appropriate. My goal was always and primarily to give voice to the voiceless.

I can't tell the young gay Egyptians who message me to come out *en masse* like I did; I don't want them to become cannon fodder for my ideals. I can't even tell them to come out to their own families; few of them had the liberalizing experiences my grandparents did, working on movies with people from all walks of life. So I tell them to be safe, to be careful, and to hang on. I try to offer them hope.

I wish I could tell the people who write me messages how long they will have to wait to feel safe in their own country. That answer will partly come down to the country's access to positive Egyptian LGBTQ representation in media; for now, such stories are censored. It will partly come down to a commitment from institutions like the World Bank to safeguard LGBTQ people by making respect for all human rights a precondition of investment.

More than anything, it will depend on the Egyptian people accepting that the tide of tolerance is inevitable. Egypt, like every nation, must decide how many lives will be lost and broken before they acknowledge that we are not faceless men but brothers, sisters, and fellow citizens.

There is nothing radical about what I am. LGBTQ people have existed in Egypt since the dawn of our great civilization. And there is nothing radical about what I want. I want to go home, quietly and safely. I want to visit the graves of my grandparents, whose funerals I was unable to attend. I want to give my country the same things my grandparents gave: my full, honest self, not as Egypt's scapegoat or its martyr, but as its patriotic son.

———

On January 1, 2019, I received lawyers' letters from several non-profit advocacy groups wishing to formally disassociate themselves from me. These were groups that I had worked with for nearly five years—organizations whose work I continue to support and admire. With them, I traveled the world and spoke on behalf of the LGBTQ community. They taught me how to be a better communicator, a better advocate, and a better human. The reason for these letters was that I had traveled to Saudi Arabia a month prior, at the invitation of the Kingdom, to experience Vision 2030, and the first international sporting event and concert in the nation's modern history.

I was hesitant to travel to Saudi Arabia because I knew full well about the Kingdom's strict adherence to Sharia and what it meant for the many LGBTQ people living there—people who risked imprisonment or death for living openly and authentically. But I also knew that an invitation from Saudi officials presented a unique opportunity to be visible and engage in an honest, albeit limited, dialogue about LGBTQ rights and HIV/AIDS policy in the region. More than that, I knew what it might mean for LGBTQ youth from the Kingdom who sent me messages daily via social channels. Seeing an openly LGBTQ person as a state-sponsored guest at a high-profile event in their country might give them hope that greater change was on the horizon. It might give them courage to hold on another day.

I was amazed at how open leading Saudi officials were about discussing the changes they sought as part of Vision 2030. I challenged them on the war in Yemen, on imprisoned and tortured female activists, and on the horrific murder of author and journalist Jamal Khashoggi. Their answers weren't always to my liking—they often seemed rehearsed and disingenuous, but they also seemed to be masking a certain internalized shame, which I found somewhat redeeming. Ultimately, I chose to attend the Formula E sporting event and the celebratory gatherings that followed and experienced a pang of hope. It was not primarily because of the government officials I sat with or the members of the royal family who greeted me, but because of the thousands of Saudi citizens who came to participate in the Kingdom's first outdoor concert featuring Western artists. It was the first time men and women would be permitted to dance together in public. As the bands started to play, the crowd cautiously swayed to the beat underneath an imposing Saudi flag, unsure of this new reality or how to respond to it. However, by the time David Guetta took the stage, men and women were fully embracing one another publicly, dancing with abandon, jumping up and down, riding on each other's shoulders—and most were crying. These were tears of joy from never experiencing this level of freedom in their own country—and from never expecting to experience it in their lifetimes. I, too, began to cry. Their joy and optimism for change was palpable—contagious. I was reminded that values, once instilled, cannot be so easily whisked away, that once people experience their first tastes of community, of love, of acceptance, of a chance to live free, there is no dam that can ever hold them back. The tides of modernization in the Kingdom are inevitable.

It was in that moment I fully understood that progress is rarely linear. It often occurs two steps forward, one step backward, particularly in a region with thousands of years of history to overcome. It's a journey down a mountainside river; it ebbs, and it flows. It can be smooth and slow and then unexpectedly rapid and turbulent. Sometimes the river even appears to turn back upon itself. The one assurance we have is that a river will continually run its track, unimpeded until it meets the sea. It's a voyage of discovery and self-discovery for which a final judgement should not be rendered midstream. This was true with my coming out, with the history of our civilization, and so it will be true of the Saudi experiment if we can maintain our optimism. You don't need to have blind faith in people, but you do need to give people a chance to prove you wrong.

I no longer consider myself an activist.

Many of the actions I see activists taking these days seem to be motivated by polarizing, all-or-nothing confrontations. A sense of pragmatism is on the decline. I get criticized for sitting at tables and engaging in difficult dialogue that yields limited results because I refuse to believe that any person is inherently bad or that anything is impossible. I get the wrath of extremists from both sides, from those who believe that my existence is an affront and from those who believe I'm selling out to the enemy. I'm okay with that. These days, I'd rather take the hits than take a side. Movements need insiders and outsiders; they need people to do the yelling and people to sit at the table—both roles are equally important. I'd much rather reach my arm across the table in the hopes of catching another, even when it is more likely that I will grasp at straws. And when a country like Saudi Arabia is making strides to change, that is the moment to hold their hand tighter—even when they make terrible mistakes. The price of letting go is far too severe; the alternative to progress is a far worse fate.

I believe in engagement and dialogue above all—in finding common ground. I seek to provide hope and inspiration. Maybe it's because I experienced and survived the downfalls of sudden revolution that I have come to appreciate a steadier rate and more managed approach to change. We cannot be afraid to compromise for some immediate, if limited, wins that could change the reality for millions of people, hoping that we might instead achieve systemic, full-scale change. I'm not suggesting that we all need to move toward the middle, but that there is an overwhelming need to find common ground, mutual respect, and empathy—these are two very different propositions.

Despite the backlash I have faced, as I write these closing words, I'm planning my return to the Kingdom. It remains a country that is perhaps the worst place on earth to be LGBTQ, a country that is one of the worst offenders of human rights and civil liberties violations. I return because, despite all the challenges and struggles I have faced, I'm still an optimist. I still believe culture can change the world, that movies will continue to open hearts and minds—and even Saudi society. Call me naive, but I will always follow Bubbie's philosophy of forgiveness and Grandfather's philosophy of leaving it all on the table, believing that the prospect of reward will always outweigh inherent risks, fear, and the greater likelihood of failure or loss.

I will continue sharing my story and staying visible for youth who still have far too few examples to look up to—reminding them that there is always hope for change. I'm just a person with a story. And I will continue to ask those listening—whether LGBTQ, ally, or stranger—to share their stories. Stories hold incredible power—power to create change, to instill empathy, and to increase acceptance—and this power lives within all of us. My story is just one of many millions, but that doesn't make it small; that's what makes it huge. We're not alone, and together, with our stories, a little optimism, and a lot of empathy, we can change the world.

ACKNOWLEDGMENTS

In writing this book I was forced to revisit much of the trauma from my past, but it equally offered me the opportunity to see how much love and support I was tendered by family and friends. Thank you for always being there.

Thank you to Elizabeth Koch, Andy Hunter, Mensah Demary, and Dan López for empowering me to share my story with the world, and to Marala Scott and Dr. Michelle Golland for helping me to find both the words and the courage.

To an extraordinary group of women who rule the world (and my heart) and who helped me find peace and home in Los Angeles—I would be lost without you: Irena Medavoy, Anne Simonds, Sybil Robson Orr, Rosanna Arquette, Kimberly Marteau Emerson, Linda Collins, Lyn Lear, DVF, RBA, Rica Rodman, Anna Lewis, Joanna Simkus Poitier, Amb. Colleen Bell, Amb. Nicole Avant, Ghada Irani, Tania Fares, Wendy Stark, Cheryl Saban, Jacqueline Emerson,

Kimberly Steward, Nona Summers, Katharine DeShaw, Lorenza Munoz, Teni Melidonian, Barbara Berkowitz, Aida Tackla O'Reilly, Carly Steel, Regina K. Scully, Angela Meng, Bahya Murad, Zoe de Givenchy, Heidi Roddenberry, Kathy Hilton, Crystal Kung Minkoff, Julia Gouw, Lorena Fuentes, Shoshana Bean, Anne Ramsay, Morgan Fairchild, Gigi Pritzker, Abby Pucker, Andrea Nevins, and Michelle Domb—the world is more beautiful because you're in it.

To mentors and friends who teach by example: Kevin Jennings, Doug Wurth, Eric Esrailian, Steven Borick, Alejandro Ramirez, Tom D'Angora, Eugenio Lopez, Mitch Ivers, Abdi Nazemian, Alan Cumming, Bob Simonds, Assi Azar, Max Mutchnick, you've given me the greatest gifts—purpose and inspiration.

Lastly, to every teacher I ever had, to every teacher out there, and to everyone who wakes up each morning determined to make the world a better place, thank you.

© Thomas Synnamon

OMAR SHARIF JR. is an Egyptian Canadian actor who currently lives in the United States. He is the grandson of Omar Sharif, the actor.